Getting Smarter Every Day

BOOK F

Grades 7–9

Created by

Dale Seymour

DALE SEYMOUR PUBLICATIONS®

Executive Editor: Catherine Anderson
Project Editor: Christine Freeman
Production/Manufacturing Director: Janet Yearian
Production/Manufacturing Manager: Karen Edmonds
Production/Manufacturing Coordinator: Joan Lee
Design Director: Phyllis Aycock
Design Manager: Jeff Kelly
Cover Design: Lynda Banks
Text Design: Nancy Carroll and Dale Seymour
Geometric Illustrations: Dale Seymour
Cartoon Illustrations: Bob Larsen
Page Composition: Alan Noyes

This book is published by Dale Seymour Publications®,
an imprint of Addison Wesley Longman, Inc.

Dale Seymour Publications

299 Jefferson Road
Parsippany, NJ 07054-0480
Customer Service: 800-872-1100

Order number DS 21915
ISBN 0-7690-0112-2

This Book Is Printed
On Recycled Paper

2 3 4 5 6 7 8 9 10-ML-04 03 02 01

Contents

Explore visual thinking, geometry, symmetry, logic, computation, factoring, and much more! Find easier worksheets up front, more adventurous worksheets further back.

Resources

Puzzles, Challenges, and Activities by Concept

Page	Puzzles, Challenges, and Activities	Computation	Geometric Relationships	Logic	Numeration	Part-Whole Relationships	Pre-Algebra	Problem Solving	Visual Thinking
1	One-Track Mind			■				■	
2	Star Designs		■						■
3	Target Practice	■					■	■	
4	Creating Number Patterns		■				■		■
5	Lines of Symmetry		■						■
6	Geometric Patterns		■						■
7	Drawing Patterns		■						■
8	Which One Differs?								■
9	Tangram Puzzle		■			■		■	■
10	Visual: Ellipse Chords	■						■	
11	Straight-Line Curves		■						■
12	Box Unfolding			■		■			■
13	Matchstick Puzzles		■			■		■	■
14	Modern Star		■						■
15	Patchwork Fractions		■		■	■		■	■
16	Impossible Tri-Bar								■
17	Divide		■		■	■	■	■	
18	Seeing Into Things		■						■
19	Logos		■						■
20	Star Designs		■						■
21	Star Designs		■			■		■	■
22	Which Post is Tallest?							■	
23	Target Practice	■					■	■	
24	Polyomino Puzzle		■					■	■
25	Cross Number Challenge	■		■	■	■	■	■	
26	Kaleidoscope Designs		■						■

Page	Puzzles, Challenges, and Activities	Computation	Geometric Relationships	Logic	Numeration	Part-Whole Relationships	Pre-Algebra	Problem Solving	Visual Thinking
27	Kaleidoscope Design		■					■	
28	Visual: Checkboard Illusion								■
29	Sum Shapes	■						■	
30	Drawing Patterns		■						■
31	Who Am I?	■		■	■		■	■	
32	Box Unfolding		■			■		■	■
33	Hidden Shapes		■					■	■
34	Photo: Sculpture		■						■
35	Tic-Tac-Number			■	■		■	■	
36	Symmetry		■						■
37	Problems to Solve		■	■				■	■
38	Star Designs		■						■
39	Creating a Design		■			■		■	■
40	Same Shapes		■					■	■
41	Target Practice	■					■	■	
42	Islamic Designs		■			■		■	■
43	Islamic Designs		■			■		■	■
44	Being Observant		■		■		■	■	■
45	Sum Shapes		■					■	
46	Regular Polygons		■						■
47	Squares in Squares	■	■					■	■
48	Basic Geometric Constructions		■					■	■
49	Can You Construct…?		■			■		■	■
50	Constructing Regular Pentagon		■					■	■
51	Fraction Puzzles				■	■		■	
52	Visual Thinking		■					■	■

Helping Young People Get Smarter Every Day

Getting Smarter Every Day is a selection of activities, puzzles, ideas, information, and graphics to excite, enrich, challenge, instruct, amaze, and entertain students. This book aims to broaden student perspectives on what mathematics really is and its application in the real world.

Numeracy and *Getting Smarter Every Day*

Wouldn't it be nice if students could "play" with numbers the way they do with balls or musical instruments? Wouldn't it be nice if students had a good feeling for what mathematics really is? Wouldn't it be nice to provide students with mathematics instruction that contributes to *numeracy*, the ability to understand and apply mathematics in everyday life?

Students often see mathematics only as arithmetic, because that is all they have been shown. They see mathematics as a series of algorithms to memorize, then apply to numbers, with a single answer as a result. Mathematics may also seem a solitary subject, without teamwork and sharing. Relatively few students explore the mathematical subjects they encounter, seeing no room for creativity.

Four major instructional approaches break through those barriers to promote numeracy, and *Getting Smarter Every Day* materials encourage and support such approaches.

Discussion and interaction. *Getting Smarter Every Day* presents puzzles that students and teachers will want to talk about. Students learn from each other. An interesting problem may have many parts; so, students with different learning styles may all experience success contributing to a group solution. When mathematics materials offer students opportunities for brainstorming, for enlightened discussion, they can discover beauty and excitement in a subject they will want to explore even further.

Active exploration. Active participation and discovery help students see the concrete aspects of mathematics, setting the stage for later generalization and abstraction. *Getting Smarter Every Day* prompts students to look for mathematical patterns in both numbers and images. When students make such discoveries themselves, they remember the relevant concepts better. Students are more likely to want to explore mathematics when they feel they have an individual role in those discoveries. Mathematics has room for creativity, for multiple methods and approaches.

Visualization and estimation. Everyday applications of mathematics frequently involve visualization and estimation. Students who are visual learners but not strong in math gain greater understanding (and enthusiasm) for mathematics through the many visual-thinking puzzles and activities in *Getting Smarter Every Day* (identified in the activity-concept grid on pages iv and v). Such selections also help students who are not skilled visual learners improve visualization skills. Though *Getting Smarter Every Day* does not specifically focus on estimation, its content involves estimating in many mathematical settings, such as probability, patterns, measurement, and visual perception. Group discussion of specific worksheets can provide many opportunities for exploring the process and value of estimation.

Interrelating concepts. Working on nonroutine, multi-step problems triggers students to use and become comfortable with a holistic approach to finding mathematical solutions. Such an approach requires teachers frequently to tie topics together. Just as a jigsaw puzzle becomes easier as more pieces fit together, so the solution of problems become easier as students connect mathematical ideas. Many materials in *Getting Smarter Every Day* involve multiple mathematical issues. The interplay of these issues is shown in the activity-concept grid on pages iv and v.

Overview of *Getting Smarter Every Day*

This is Book F in a series of six books in the *Getting Smarter Every Day series*. This book is designed for students of varying ability levels in grades 7 through 9. Mathematical prerequisites are, for the most part, basic. (For activities more suitable for students not working up to grade level or ability, also look at Book E.)

Getting Smarter Every Day Book F contains approximately 100 worksheets. They are not intended for use page-by-page in numerical sequence. Rather, "pick and choose," selecting activities for a specific purpose. In general, the difficulty of activities increases from the front of the book to the back. The topics and concepts included often do not appear in regular classroom texts and, admittedly, are favorites of the author. The broad concepts included are:

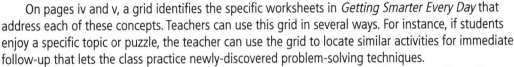

- computation
- geometric relationships
- logic
- numeration

- part-whole relationships
- pre-algebra
- problem solving
- visual thinking

On pages iv and v, a grid identifies the specific worksheets in *Getting Smarter Every Day* that address each of these concepts. Teachers can use this grid in several ways. For instance, if students enjoy a specific topic or puzzle, the teacher can use the grid to locate similar activities for immediate follow-up that lets the class practice newly-discovered problem-solving techniques.

For even more activities on a topic, *Getting Smarter Every Day* also includes More Smart Books (pages 118 and 119), a list of specific books with related worksheets. This list is keyed to the specific worksheets in this book. Also look at Smart Math Web Sites, on page 120.

Worksheet completion time for the average student varies but generally ranges from 15 to 45 minutes. Perceived difficulty will vary considerably, as ability also ranges considerably in most mathematics classes in this grade range. For a more specific estimate of time requirement, and to assess appropriateness of a worksheet for a specific class, try an activity before assigning it.

Ways to Use This Book

This book is a resource whose pages teachers may use as blackline masters to reproduce worksheets for their own classroom or for specific students. Teachers may also use these pages to create overhead transparencies.

Warmups. *Getting Smarter Every Day* worksheet pages serve nicely as warmup handouts or overhead transparencies. The teacher may give the students five to ten minutes to work on an activity (while handling attendance and homework collection), then have a brief class discussion on questions, ambiguities, and strategies. If needed, the class may complete the worksheet during class time or as regular or optional homework.

Enrichment. In a typical class, student ability and interest spread is amazing. The teacher then faces quite a task to challenge each student. *Getting Smarter Every Day* worksheets serve well as "selected activities" for specific students.

Introduction to a new topic. If students have become accustomed to the style and pace of their mathematics textbook, they may expect the next chapter to feel just like the one preceding it, holding little excitement. As a surprise, teachers can grab student attention by using a relevant problem, puzzle, or activity from *Getting Smarter Every Day*. The challenge of a puzzle often has more motivational appeal than, "Now, turn to page…"

Extension or review of a concept. Teachers may use *Getting Smarter Every Day* worksheets to give students extra practice or review of a textbook topic. The worksheets may also provide an application of or connection with a recently-studied topic. A great way to extend a topic is to have students make a problem or a puzzle of their own. Several puzzle formats in this book lend themselves to that kind of extension. Often, students really understand a concept for the first time when they create their own problem.

Bulletin boards. Several pages in *Getting Smarter Every Day* present a graphic image without an activity assignment. Photocopies (perhaps at an enlarged scale) of these images make intriguing bulletin board materials. You may also display copies of such images that students have colored, outlined, or otherwise modified to display a variety of patterns within such images.

Assessing Student Results in *Getting Smarter Every Day*

Though *Getting Smarter Every Day* emphasizes thinking and process, teachers (and students) often want to know the "right" answer to puzzles and challenges. Experience with these materials will show that sometimes, even in mathematics, there is more than one "right" answer.

Answers. Solutions are provided in Smart Answers, starting on page 111. For many of the problems in *Getting Smarter Every Day,* answers are not unique. Praise students who get different answers, if their answers are correct. Use such experiences to help students see that, in the real world, a problem often has more than one correct answer. To extend a good problem, ask, "Is the answer unique?".

To grade or not to grade. Students, particularly students who have a low opinion of mathematics and of their own mathematics ability, often find refreshing math activities that are different, fun, and not graded. Students with an interest in art, for example, who begin to see math applications in art may have an attitudinal change towards mathematics. Students who are not graded on *every* thing they do may welcome the freedom from fear of failure.

Using Special Features in *Getting Smarter Every Day*

Getting Smarter Every Day includes several types of material that present opportunities for exploring mathematics visually without specific assignments.

Grids and dot paper. Many worksheets in *Getting Smarter Every Day* emphasize drawing, sketching, designing, or problem solving. Fun Grids to Copy and Use, starting on page 102, provides several grid and dot masters. Students can use copies of these grids to work on such activities, especially to try extensions on their own. If you do not provide such grids with specific worksheets, let students know that they may request such grids if they want to use them.

Graphic images. Graphic images in *Getting Smarter Every Day* with no specific task assignment are designed to foster student appreciation of the beauty of mathematics. As previously suggested, you may use these as bulletin board material. You may also use such a graphic as a "prop" to ask students to bring in images from magazines, posters, or newspapers. From these contributions, you may create a bulletin board on architecture, sculpture, art, nature, and their connections to mathematics. Over the years, you may accumulate impressive files of pictures that reveal this beauty to your students.

Use of design technology. All the geometric designs in this book were created by the author on the computer using Adobe Illustrator® software. Most computers have some drawing programs. You may use the graphics in *Getting Smarter Every Day* as models for students to create related images with computer drawing programs or by hand.

ONE -TRACK MIND

Last Saturday at Eureka Fields Race Track:

In Race 1:

    Horse A beat D. E beat F. C beat E.
    F beat D. B came in third, and B beat A.
    Which horse won Race 1? _____

In Race 2:

* No horse finished next to a horse with
  the letter of the alphabet next to its own.
* A finished in front of C.
* D won the race.
* F came in third.
* B finished ahead of A and E.
* E came in last.

In the boxes below, give the order of the finish of all six horses in Race 2.

1st	2nd	3rd	4th	5th	6th
☐	☐	☐	☐	☐	☐

STAR DESIGNS

In the design below, each successive star is reduced by the "golden section ratio."

MATHEMATICS IS THE STUDY OF PATTERN

TARGET PRACTICE

Write a number sentence that hits the target.
For each problem, use each of the numbers
in the squares once. Use no other numbers.
Use any math symbols you choose.

 9   3   12

Use these numbers in each sentence for problems 1–4.

Example: If the target were 13, a solution would be: (12 ÷ 3) + 9 = 13.

1. _____ = 4   2. _____ = 15

3. _____ = 5   4. _____ = 36

 12   2   14

Use these numbers in each sentence for problems 5–8.

5. _____ = 5   6. _____ = 1

7. _____ = 20   8. _____ = 10

CREATING NUMBER PATTERNS

For this table of numbers, each row follows a rule. The rule appears in the black hexagon at the left of the row. At the head of each column is the value for the number (*n*) to use. Fill in each blank hexagon, using the corresponding rule and value for *n*. (Remember to do what's in parentheses first.)

rule	$n=1$	$n=2$	$n=3$	$n=4$	$n=5$	$n=6$	$n=7$
1. $n+3$		5					
2. $2n-1$				7			
3. $5n$						30	
4. $3n+2$							
5. $3n^2$							
6. n^3	1						
7. $\dfrac{2n-1}{2}$					4.5		
8. $\dfrac{n(n+1)}{2}$							

LINES OF SYMMETRY

If a shape cut out of paper can be folded in half on a straight line to fit exactly onto the other half, then that shape has symmetry. This kind of symmetry is called **reflective symmetry** or **bilateral symmetry**. The fold line is called the **line of symmetry**.

Most of the shapes on this page have **reflective symmetry**. In many cases, in fact, the shape can be folded in more than one place to fit onto itself. For instance, an equilateral triangle has three lines of symmetry.

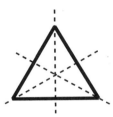 Equilateral triangle
(3 equal sides)
Dotted lines are lines of symmetry.

Draw in all lines of symmetry on each of these shapes.

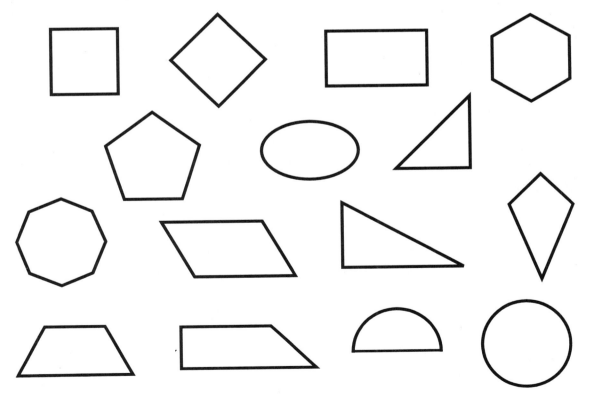

GEOMETRIC PATTERNS

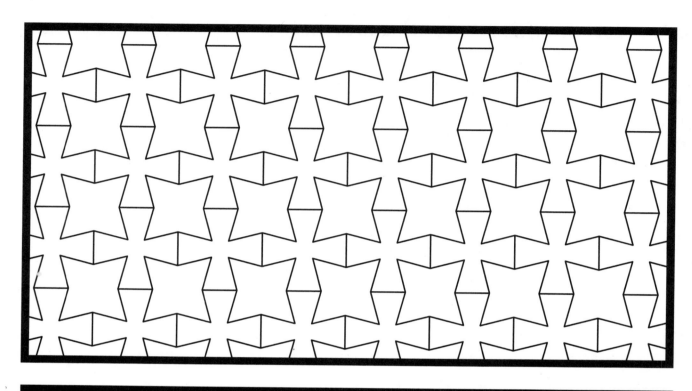

DRAWING PATTERNS

Continue each drawing pattern.

1.

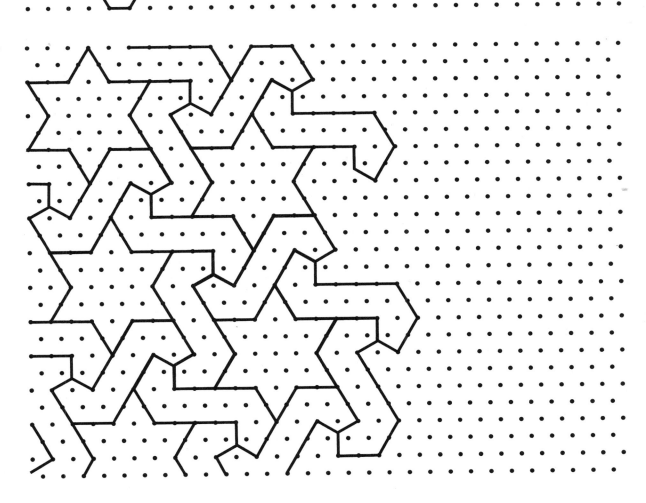

2.

WHICH ONE DIFFERS?

In each problem, circle the one shape that is different some way.

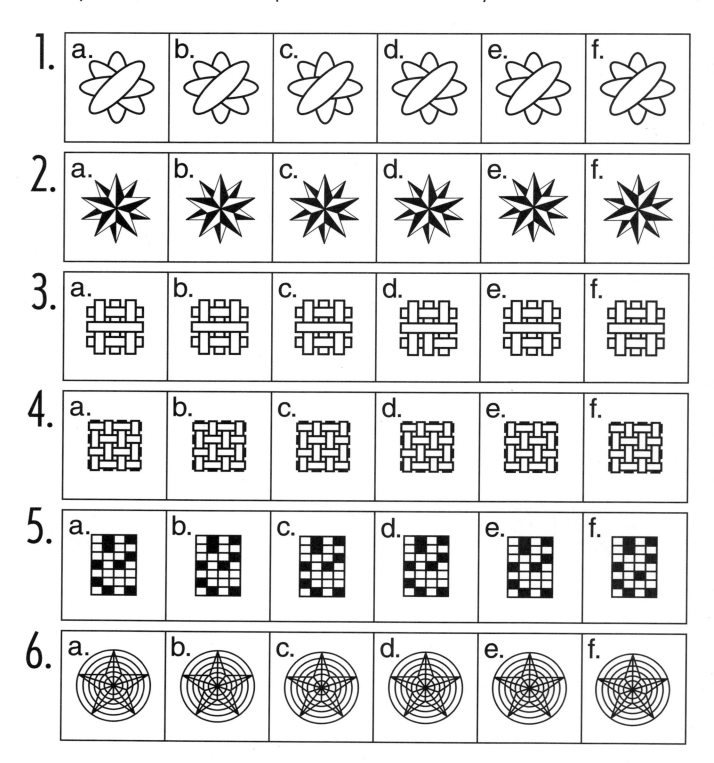

TANGRAM PUZZLE

Have a copy of this page made. Cut out each of the seven shapes below and place the pieces together in the shape of a square. You can also make many other geometric shapes, animals, people, boats, etc., using all seven pieces. This Chinese puzzle is many centuries old.

STRAIGHT-LINE CURVES

You can draw curves by drawing all straight lines.
Here's how. Use a ruler with a straight edge.
Connect all points six sections apart with straight
line segments. To create another curve inside
this same circle, then connect all points nine
sections apart. Finally, connect all points, on
this circle, twelve sections apart. Your finished
image should look like the graphic to the right.

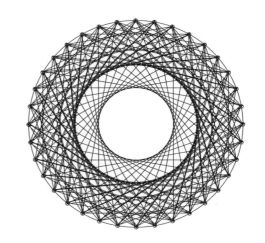

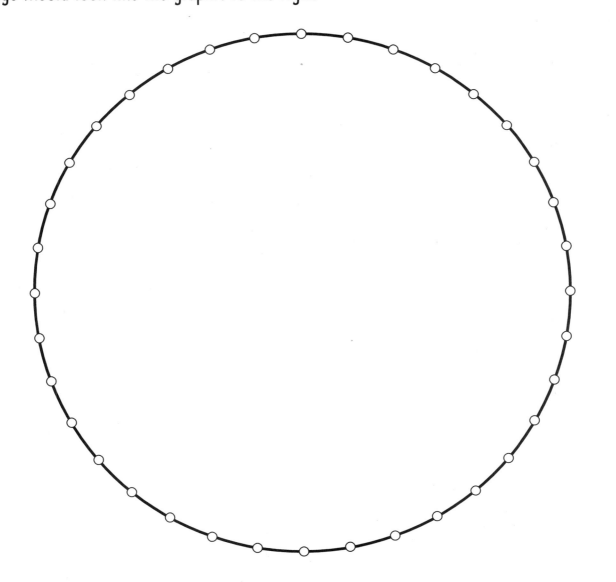

BOX UNFOLDING

Imagine that the box at the left of each problem is unfolded into a pattern. Which of the four patterns make the box shown? It may help to cut out your own pattern.

1.

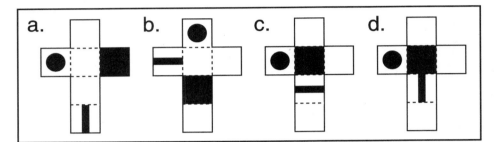

2.

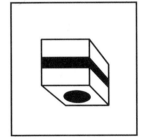

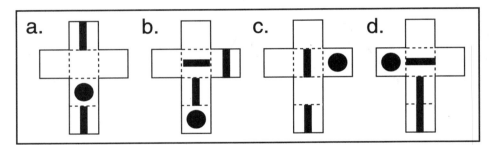

3.

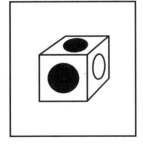

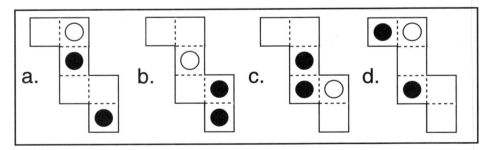

4.

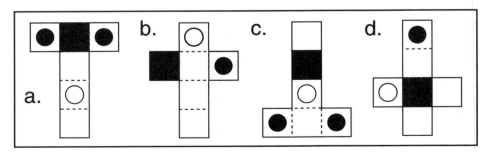

MATCHSTICK PUZZLES

Sketch your answer in the space provided.

1. Move four matches and make three equilateral triangles.

2. How can you arrange six matches to form four equilateral triangles?

3. Move four matches to make four congruent squares.

GEOMETRIC PATTERNS IN QUILTS: MODERN STAR

PATCHWORK FRACTIONS

What fractional part of each patchwork quilt square shown below is white?

1.

_____

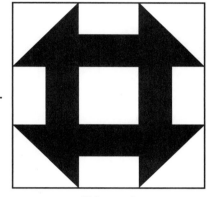

Wrench

2.

_____

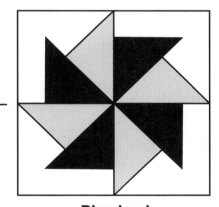

Pinwheel

3.

_____

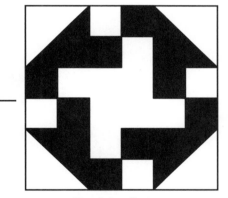

Prairie Queen

4.

_____

Indian Puzzle
(Chinese Coin & Monkey Wrench)

5.

_____

Cross and Crown

The impossible tri-bar can be drawn from a series of tessellating equilateral triangles as shown above.

DIVIDE

Draw **three** line segments that divide a circle into:

4 parts	5 parts	6 parts
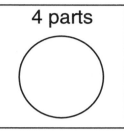	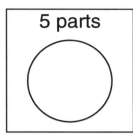	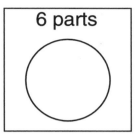

7 parts	3 parts	2 parts
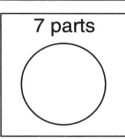	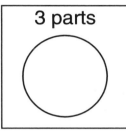	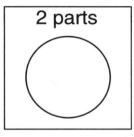

Draw **four** line segments that divide a circle into:

5 parts	6 parts	7 parts
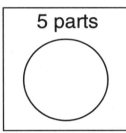	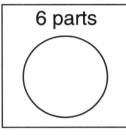	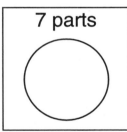

8 parts	9 parts	10 parts
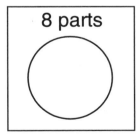	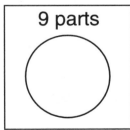	

What is the maximum number of parts that a circle can be divided into with n line segments? Be careful. This one is tricky!

segments	1	2	3	4	5	...	n
parts	__	__	__	__	__		_____

SEEING INTO THINGS

Steps in making letter stars: 1. Type a letter.   2. Skew the letter 40°.   3. Reflect & copy.
4. Rotate 72°.   5. Rotate 72°.   6. Rotate 72°.   7. Rotate 72°.   8. Rotate to vertical.

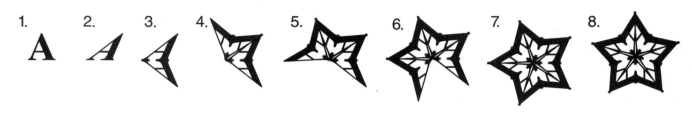

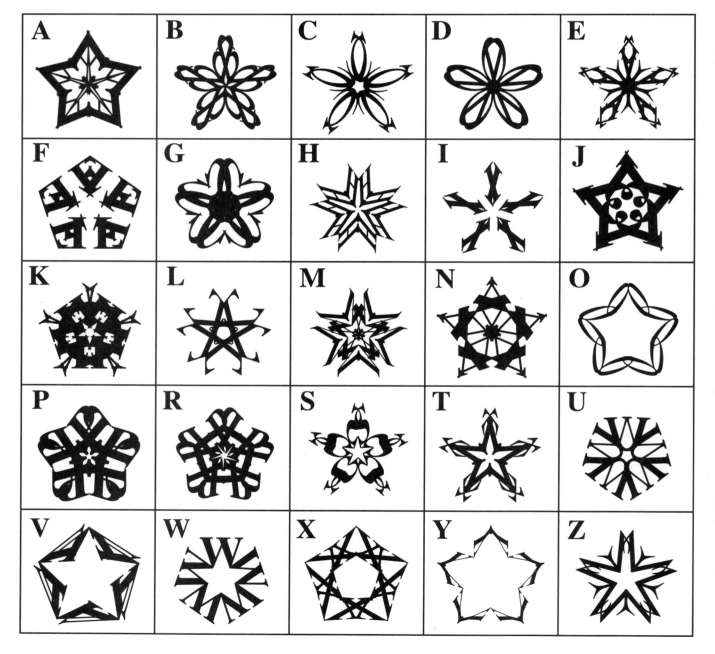

LOGOS

Logos are designs that identify a product or company. Logos are often geometric. Designers frequently design logos to be simple and symmetrical. Sometimes the company's initials or their products are in the logo.

Here are some examples of typical logos.

Simple, Symmetric Geometric

Company's Initials

Company's Product or Name

Combinations

Look through newspapers and magazine to find ten good examples of the properties shown above. Design a logo of your own.

STAR DESIGNS

STAR DESIGNS

Use these patterns to create your own star designs.

Which post is the tallest?
Are you sure?
Measure them.

TARGET PRACTICE

Write a number sentence that hits the target.
For each problem, use each of the numbers
in the squares once. Use no other numbers.
Use any math symbols you choose.

1. _____ =  10

 3 6 2 5

2. _____ = 5

 3 6 2 5

3. _____ = 25

 3 6 2 5

4. _____ = 20

POLYOMINO PUZZLE

Polyominoes are shapes made from squares. Polyominoes made from five squares are called **pentominoes**. Five pentamino shapes are given below. Have a copy of this page made. Cut out the black shapes and try to fit all five on the 5 X 5 square.

It's OK to flip the pieces over.

CROSS NUMBER CHALLENGE

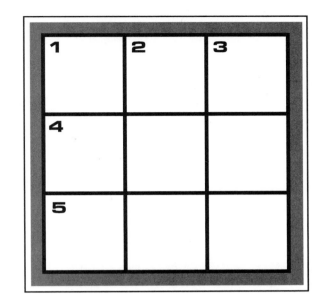

ACROSS

1. It's an even number. It has two prime factors.
   The first digit is twice the difference between the second two.
4. An even number, it is divisible by nine.
   Its prime factorization contains five digits.
   The first digit equals the sum of the second and third.
5. It's an odd number, divisible by seven. Its digits are in descending order.

DOWN

1. It's an odd number. It has three two-digit palindromic factors. It has only two unique prime factors.
2. The sum of its digits divides the number evenly. The sum of the first two digits equals the third. One factorization can be written as a four-digit palindrome.
3. It's divisible by three. One of its two proper factors is a three-digit prime. All three digits divide the product of the second and third.

DIAGONALLY

1. It's divisible by three. It has two prime factors. Each of its digits divides the sum of its three digits.
3. It's divisible by three. It has two prime factors. The sum of the second and third digits is twice the first digit.

**Kaleidoscope designs are made
from mirror reflections.**

KALEIDOSCOPE DESIGN

A kaleidoscope design contains mirror symmetry on each of the three lines connecting opposite vertices of the regular hexagons. Design some kaleidoscope patterns of your own in the grids provided.

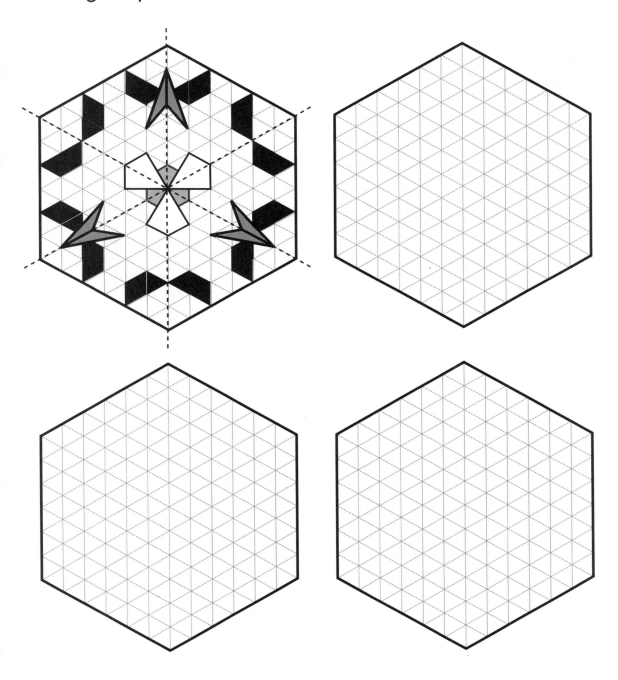

SUM SHAPES

This is a sum side. Its sum is 14. You can use sum sides to build sum shapes.

In each of the following problems, use numbers 0, 1, 2, 3, 4, 5, 6, 7, 8 or 9 to make the sum. Don't use the same number twice in one problem.

1. Make a sum shape of 14 on each side.

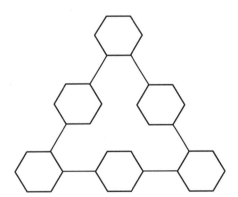

2. Make a sum shape of 15 on each side.

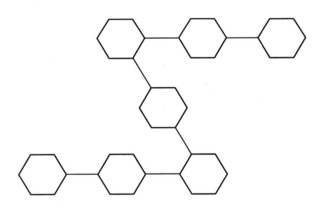

3. Make a sum shape of 16 on each side.

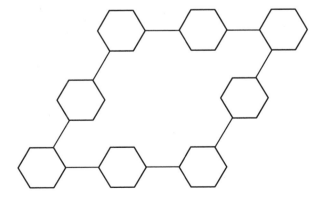

4. Make a sum shape of 17 on each side.

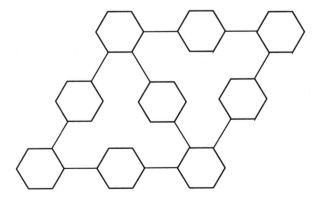

DRAWING PATTERNS

Continue the drawing pattern.

WHO AM I?

1. I am the largest three-digit number that is divisible by each of the first three prime numbers.
Who am I?

2. I am a two-digit number. I'm the product of two consecutive integers. The sum of my digits is greater than the product of my digits. Both my digits are even.
Who am I?

3. I am a three-digit square number. The sum of my digits is the same as the sum of the digits of my square root. The product of my three digits is one less than my square root.
Who am I?

4. I am a member of the Even Number Club. The product of my three digits is 28. The sum of my digits is 12. The product of my hundreds digit and my units digit is less than my tens digit.
Who am I?

EVEN NUMBERS CLUB MEMBER ?

5. I am an odd number. Are you? Each of my three digits is different. My average digit size is 5, but 5 is not one of my digits. The product of my digits is less than 45. My three digits have no common factors.
Who am I?

BOX UNFOLDING

Imagine that the box at the left of each problem is unfolded in a cross pattern. Which of the four patterns make the box shown? It may help to cut out your own pattern.

1.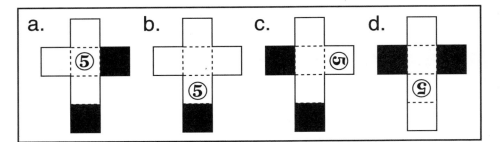
   a.   b.   c.   d.

2.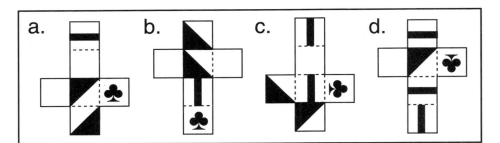
   a.   b.   c.   d.

3.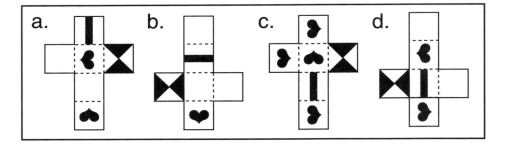
   a.   b.   c.   d.

4.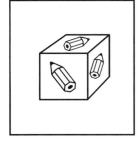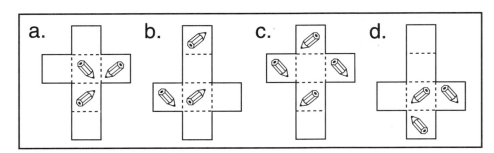
   a.   b.   c.   d.

HIDDEN SHAPES

Hidden in these "pick-up-sticks" are a regular hexagon, a regular pentagon, and a regular octagon. Can you find them? Outline or shade them in.

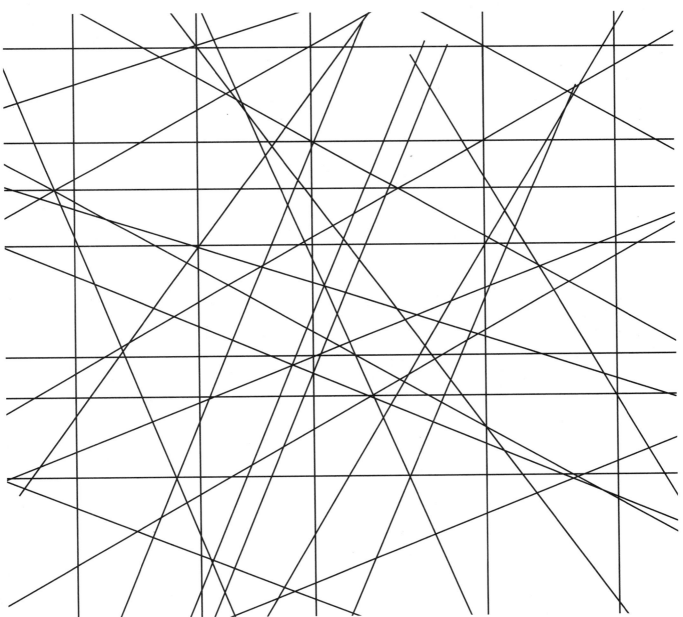

Immortality by John Robinson
Used by permission of Edition Limitée.

TIC-TAC-NUMBER

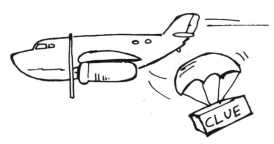

Use the clues to fill in the nine squares in each problem with digits 1–9 (one digit per square).

1.

a. The four corner numbers are prime.
b. The middle column contains all square numbers.
c. 2 and 3 are in the top row.
d. 4 is located in the bottom row.
e. 5 and 6 are in the left column.
f. The center number is smaller than the number directly above it.

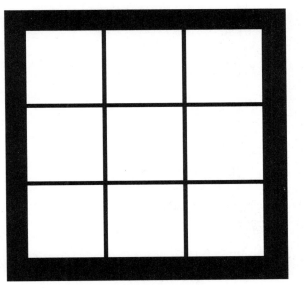

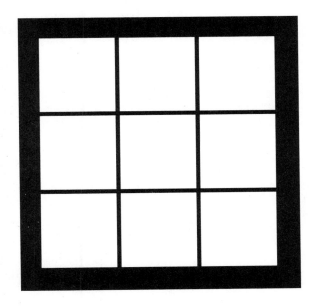

2.

a. 7 and 1 are in the top row.
b. 9 and 6 are in the middle row.
c. 5 and 8 are in the bottom row.
d. 6 and 4 are in the left column.
e. 1 and 2 are in the center column.
f. 5 and 3 are in the right column.
g. 3 is a corner number.

SYMMETRY

YRTEMMYS
SYMMETRY

Each of the three designs is symmetrical. Notice that one half has been reflected across the dotted vertical or horizontal line shown.

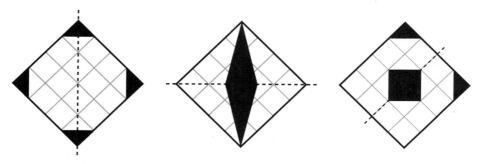

Complete each design below by reflecting it across the dotted line shown.

PROBLEMS TO SOLVE

1. Form exactly two squares by drawing:

   a. five line segments   b. six line segments   c. seven line segments

2. Of 200 coins, 199 are the same weight and one is lighter than the others. Explain how you could use a balance scale to identify the lighter coin in no more than five weighings.

3. What is the angle between the minute hand and the hour hand at 3:20?

STAR DESIGNS

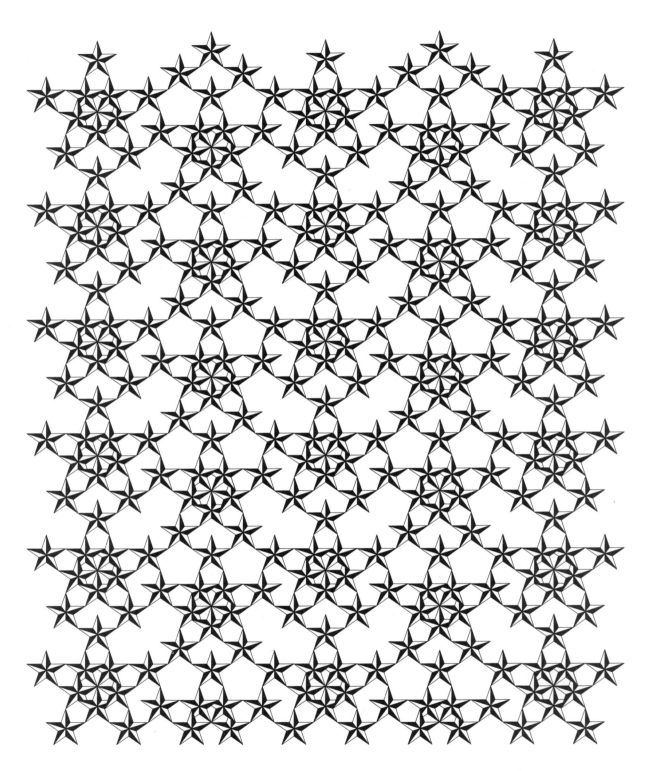

MATHEMATICS IS THE STUDY OF PATTERN

CREATING A DESIGN

The steps below show how a designer makes a five-pointed star.

1. Draw a circle.	**2.** Draw a radius of the circle.	**3.** Rotate the radius 1/5 of a complete rotation (72°).
4. Repeat the rotation, dividing circle into fifths.	**5.** Erase the circle. It was only a helper.	**6.** Connect the endpoints of all non-adjacent radii.
7. Extend each of the five radii.	**8.** Erase lines.	**9.** Fill in every other triangle, and rotate figure.

SAME SHAPES

In each problem, find the three pairs of shapes that are exactly the same.

_____ & _____ / _____ & _____ / _____ & _____   _____ & _____ / _____ & _____ / _____ & _____

1.
a.	b.	c.
d.	e.	f.
g.	h.	i.
j.	k.	l.
m.	n.	o.
p.	q.	r.
s.	t.	u.
v.	w.	x.
y.	z.	*

2.
a.	b.	c.
d.	e.	f.
g.	h.	i.
j.	k.	l.
m.	n.	o.
p.	q.	r.
s.	t.	u.
v.	w.	x.
y.	z.	*

TARGET PRACTICE

Using each of the four numbers in the squares once, write a number sentence for each problem. Use any math symbols you choose.

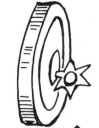

◆ 4 ◆ 6 ◆ 3 ◆ 12 ◆

1. _____ = ⓪	7. _____ = ⑥
2. _____ = ①	8. _____ = ⑦
3. _____ = ②	9. _____ = ⑧
4. _____ = ③	10. _____ = ⑨
5. _____ = ④	11. _____ = ⑩
6. _____ = ⑤	12. _____ = ⑪

ISLAMIC DESIGNS

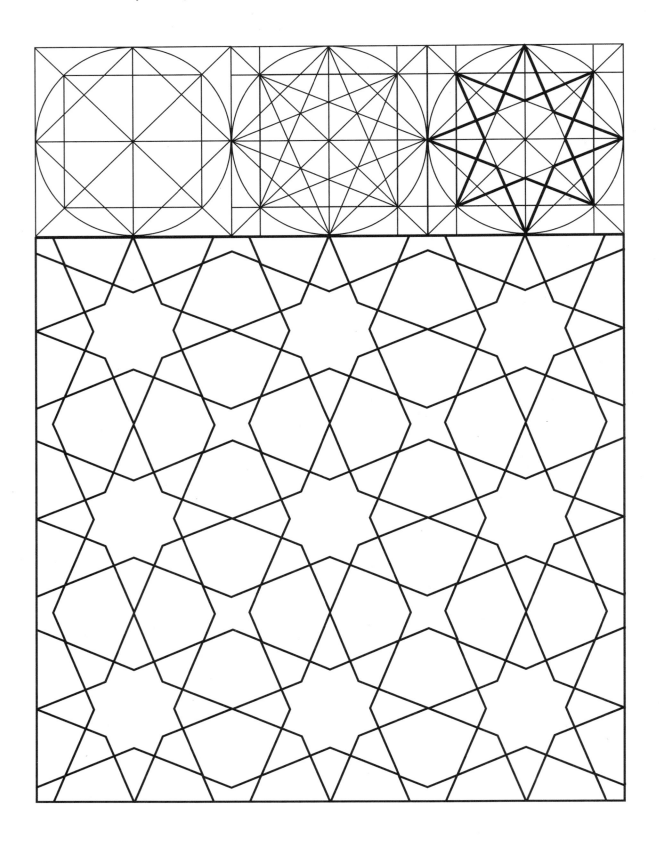

ISLAMIC DESIGNS

Use this grid to form a design of your own.

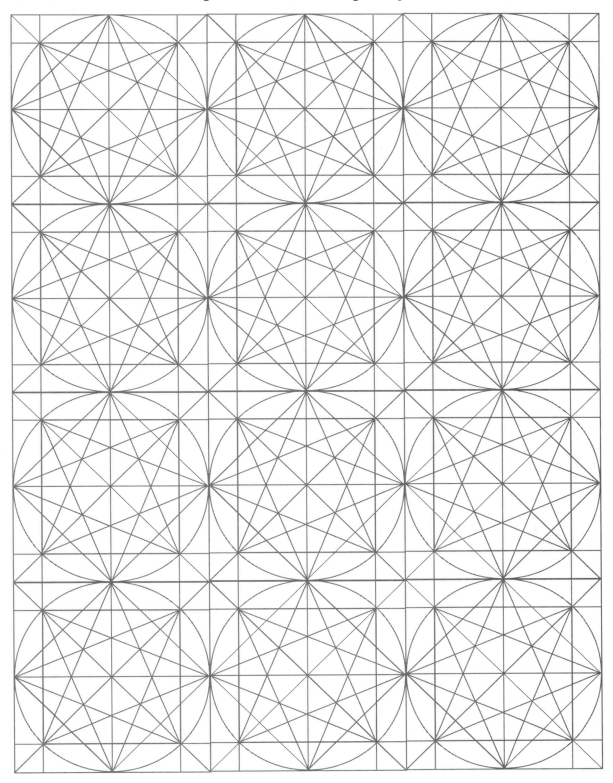

BEING OBSERVANT

What do we have in common?

More than one answer may be correct.

1.
243
729
3
27
2187
81

2.
12
30
72
42
56
156
20

3.
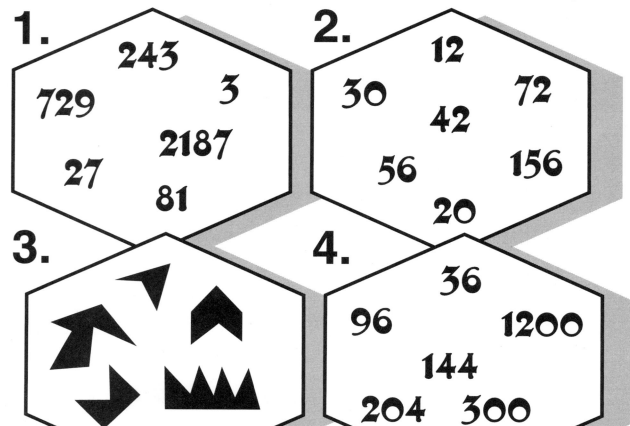

4.
36
96
1200
144
204   300

5.
144
55
3
1
34   13

6.
36
15
6
55
91
105

SUM SHAPES

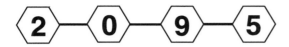

This is a sum side. Its sum is 16. You can use sum sides to build sum shapes.

In each of the following problems, use numbers 0, 1, 2, 3, 4, 5, 6, 7, 8 or 9 to make the sum. Don't use the same number twice in one problem.

1. Make a sum shape of 17 on each side.

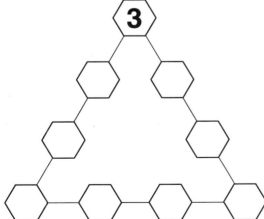

2. Make a sum shape of 17 on each side.

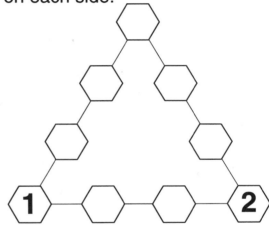

3. Make a sum shape of 19 on each side.

4. Make a sum shape of 20 on each side.

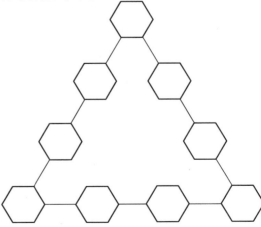

Regular Polygons

A *polygon* is a closed figure whose sides are line segments. A *regular polygon* is one all of whose angles are congruent (equal) and all of whose sides are congruent (equal). Some polygon names are given below:

triangle	square	pentagon	hexagon
septagon or heptagon	octagon	nonagon	decagon
undecagon	dodecagon	13-gon	14-gon
15-gon	16-gon	17-gon	18-gon
19-gon	20-gon	100-gon	

SQUARES IN SQUARES

1. How does the area of each square compare with the area of the next smaller square? _____

2. How do the areas of every second square compare? _____

3. How does the perimeter of each square compare with the perimeter of the next smaller square? _____

4. If the length of one side of the largest square is *n*, what is the length of one side of the next-to-largest square? _____

5. If the largest square is #1, what number is the square whose area would be 1/64th the area of square #1? _____

BASIC GEOMETRIC CONSTRUCTIONS

Copied line segment	Bisection of a line segment
 $\overline{AB} \cong \overline{CD}$	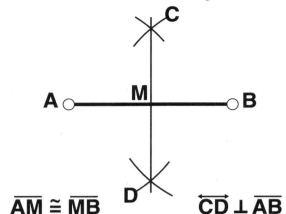 $\overline{AM} \cong \overline{MB}$ $\overrightarrow{CD} \perp \overline{AB}$

Construction of a perpendicular to a line from a point off the line	Construction of a perpendicular to a line from a point on the line
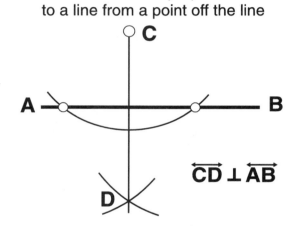 $\overleftrightarrow{CD} \perp \overleftrightarrow{AB}$	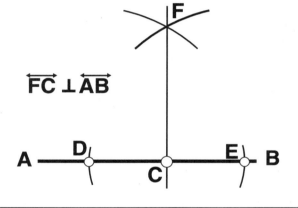 $\overleftrightarrow{FC} \perp \overleftrightarrow{AB}$

Bisection of an angle	Copied angle
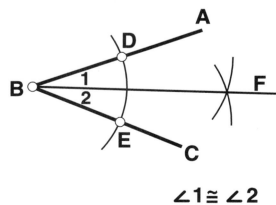 $\angle 1 \cong \angle 2$	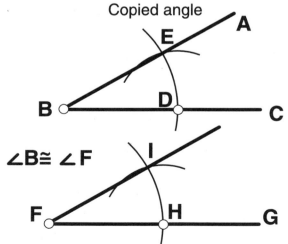 $\angle B \cong \angle F$

CAN YOU CONSTRUCT THESE?

Use either compass and straightedge or a computer drawing program.

CONSTRUCTING A REGULAR PENTAGON

1. Draw a circle and a diameter of that circle, **AB**.

2. Construct another diameter, **CD**, the perpendicular bisector of **AB**.

3. Bisect **OB**. Label the midpoint **M**.

4. Using **M** as a center and **CM** as a radius, draw an arc intersecting **AO** at **E**.

5. **CE** is the required length of one side of the inscribed regular pentagon.

6. On the circle, mark five arcs with radius **CE.** Connect their intersections to form the regular pentagon.

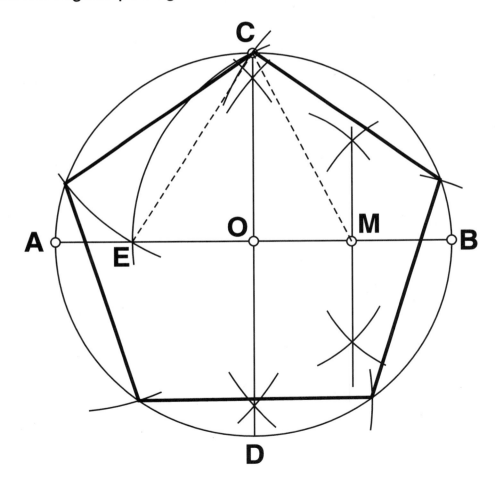

FRACTION PUZZLES

Fill in the fraction value for each open circle on each number line. For each puzzle, use each boxed digit in that puzzle once. One example has been done for you.

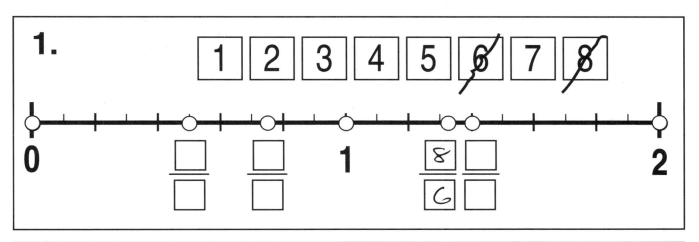

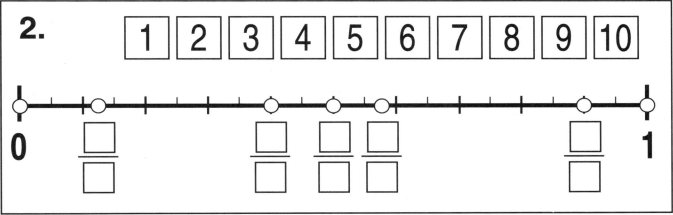

VISUAL THINKING

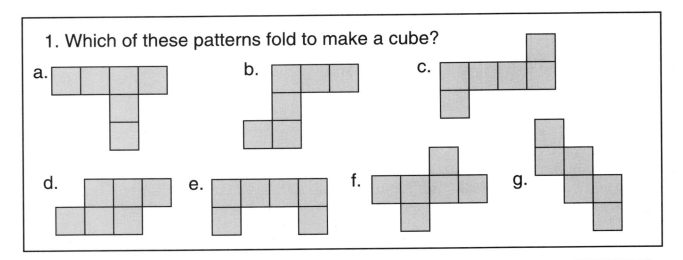

1. Which of these patterns fold to make a cube?

a.

b.

c.

d.

e.

f.

g.

2. What do these reflected sentences say?

a. .sint bɒɘɿ nɒɔ I

b. .bniw ɘʜɟ ɘʞil nuЯ

c. .ǫnivɘilɘd si ǫniɘɘᕢ

d. .ɘm oɟ ʏnnuʇ ʞool ꙅɿɘɟɟɘl ɘmoꙅ

3. If you follow steps 1 through 5, which shape results when you unfold the paper?

1. crease   2. fold   3. crease   4. fold   5. punch

a.   b.   c.   d.   e.

a.   b.   c.   d.

TARGET PRACTICE

Using each of the four numbers in the squares
once, write a number sentence for each problem.
Use any math symbols you choose.

1. = **0**	7. = **6**
2. = **1**	8. = **7**
3. = **2**	9. = **8**
4. = **3**	10. = **9**
5. = **4**	11. = **10**
6. = **13**	12. = **11**

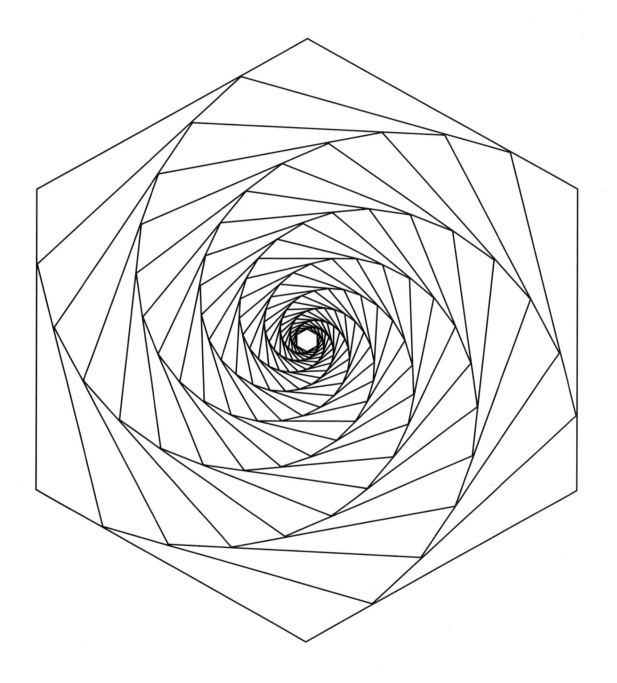

GEOMETRIC RELATIONSHIPS

Describe each relationship, using the best of these phrases:

is always / can be / is never

1. A polygon _____ a quadrilateral.

2. A square _____ a rectangle.

3. A parallelogram _____ a quadrilateral.

4. A rhombus _____ a square.

5. A rectangle _____ a parallelogram.

6. A quadrilateral _____ a rhombus.

7. A trapezoid _____ a parallelogram.

8. A square _____ a trapezoid.

9. A rectangle _____ a quadrilateral.

10. A quadrilateral _____ a polygon.

11. A rhombus _____ a rectangle.

12. A square _____ a parallelogram.

13. A parallelogram _____ a rhombus.

14. A square _____ a rhombus.

15. A rhombus _____ a parallelogram.

SQUARE & HEXAGON PUZZLE

Have a copy of this page made. Cut out each of the five shapes below and place the pieces together in the shape of a square. You can also make a hexagon with the same five pieces.

JUGGLING DIGITS

To solve certain problems it is important to be able to make an organized list of digits.

1. Make an organized list of **all** three-digit numbers greater than 300 whose digit sum is 7.

| 3 | 0 | |

| 3 | | |

2. Make an organized list of **all** three-digit odd numbers less than 450 whose digit sum is 10.

| 1 | | |

3. Make an organized list of **all** three-digit even numbers greater than 500 whose digit sum is 20.

4. What is the largest three-digit multiple of 5 whose digit sum is 20? _____

Photo source: LeRoy Dalton

Digit Dilemmas

1. What three digits (not necessarily different) can be arranged to form two different three-digit squares?

2. Find the four two-digit numbers that meet both of the following requirements:
* The product of two primes.
* If quadrupled, still a two-digit number.

3. What do all the two-digit numbers have in common whose digit sum is two less than their digit difference?

4. Find the smallest two-digit number that can be obtained by reversing the order of a three-digit number and then subtracting it from the original three-digit number.

SAME SHAPES

Which five pairs are exactly the same?

_____ and _____   _____ and _____

_____ and _____   _____ and _____

_____ and _____

1.	2.	3.	4.	5.
6.	7.	8.	9.	10.
11.	12.	13.	14.	15.
16.	17.	18.	19.	20.
21.	22.	23.	24.	25.
26.	27.	28.	29.	30.

ALPHA-NUMERIC PUZZLES

Alpha-numeric puzzles are computation problems written in letters instead of numerals. To make a solution, you'll need to figure out which numeral each letter represents. If a letter appears more than once, it represents the same number. One puzzle may have several different correct answers.

1.

```
 FOUR
+FOUR
─────
EIGHT
```

2.

```
THREE
+FOUR
─────
SEVEN
```

3.

```
  ONE
  TWO
 +SIX
─────
 NINE
```

4.

```
  ADD
  FOR
 + DE
─────
  SUM
```

GEOMETRIC PATTERNS

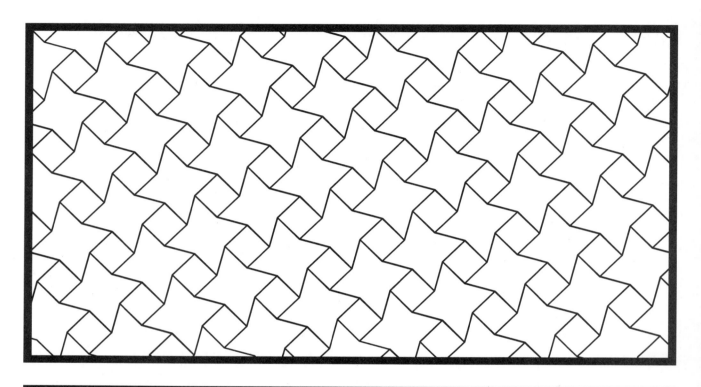

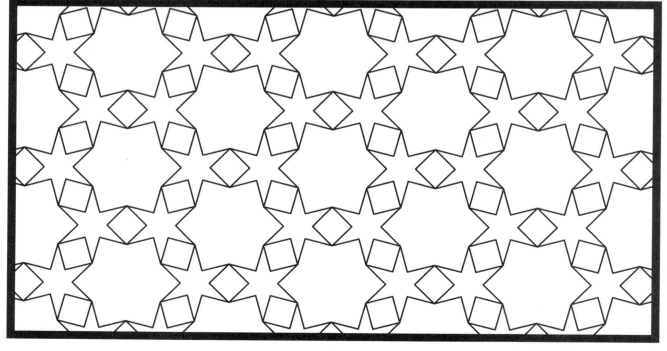

GEO-MATCH

Find the match for each of the 20 geometric shapes listed at the right. <u>Do not use a number twice.</u>

a.	b.	c.	d.
e.	f.	g.	h.
i.	j.	k.	l.
m.	n.	o.	p.
q.	r.	s.	t.
u.	v.	w.	x.

____ 1. scalene triangle
____ 2. square
____ 3. rhombus
____ 4. rectangle
____ 5. trapezoid
____ 6. isosceles triangle
____ 7. equilateral triangle
____ 8. isosceles trapezoid
____ 9. quadrilateral
____ 10. heptagon
____ 11. decagon
____ 12. octagon
____ 13. right triangle
____ 14. kite
____ 15. ellipse
____ 16. pentagon
____ 17. regular pentagon
____ 18. parallelogram
____ 19. hexagon
____ 20. regular hexagon

SYMMETRY IN DESIGN

The 20 designs shown below are all more than 100 years old. People had their initials placed on jewelry and other personal belongings. Designers tried to form the initials so that the letters shared parts. They often made the designs quite symmetrical. What letters do you see in each design? Write your answers in the blanks at the right.

1.
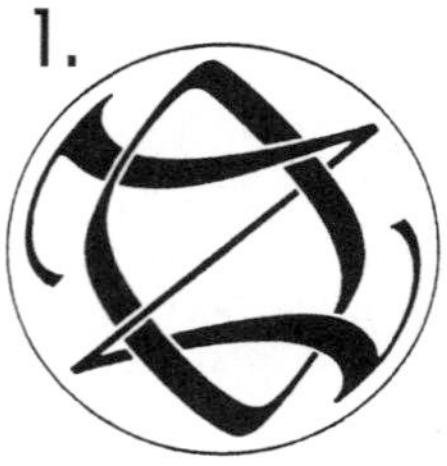

2.
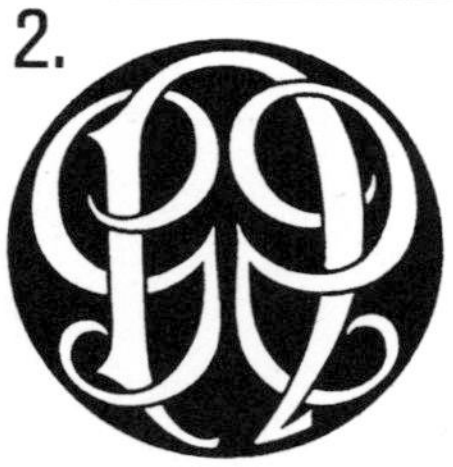

3.
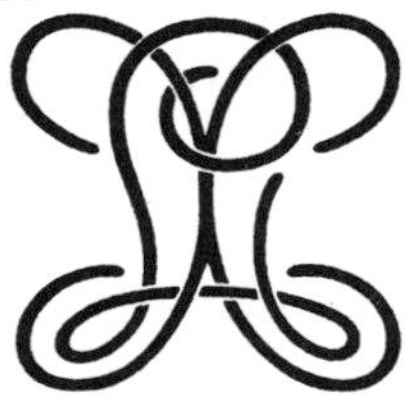

4.
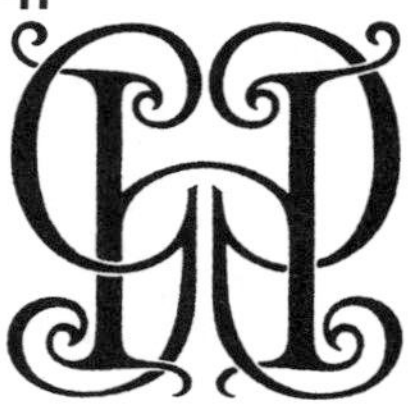

5.
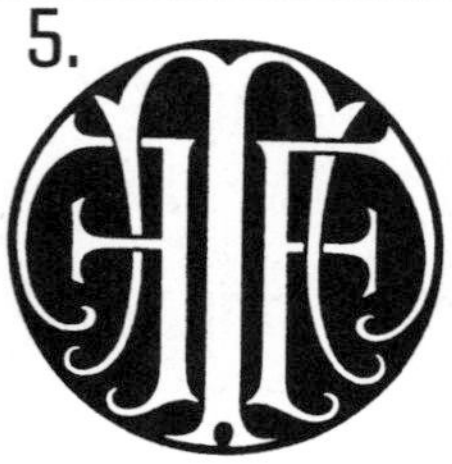

6.
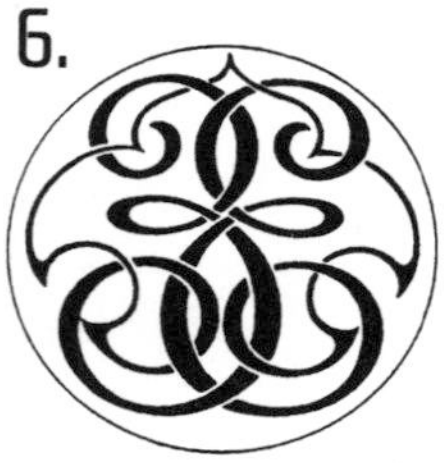

7.
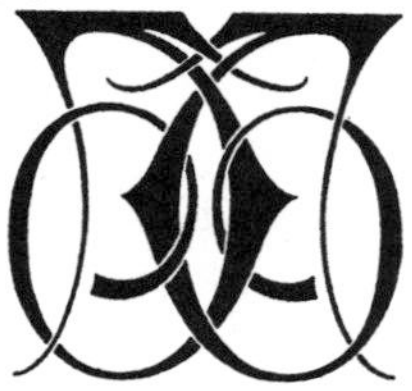

8.
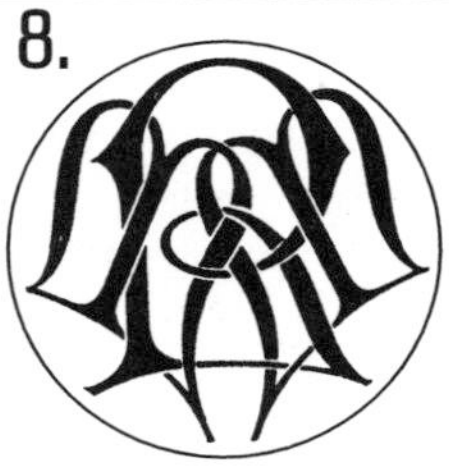

9.
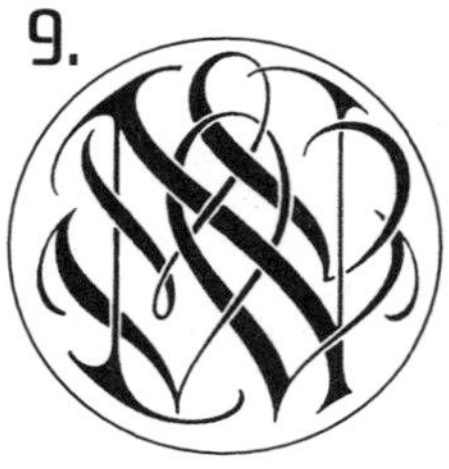

10.
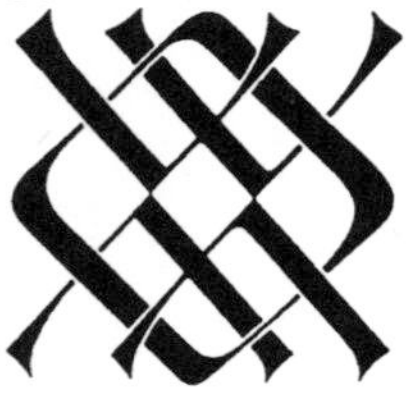

11.
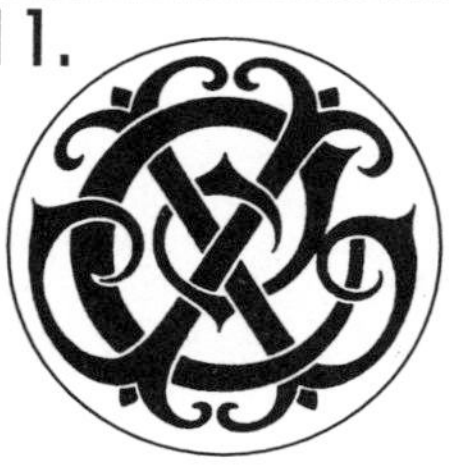

12.
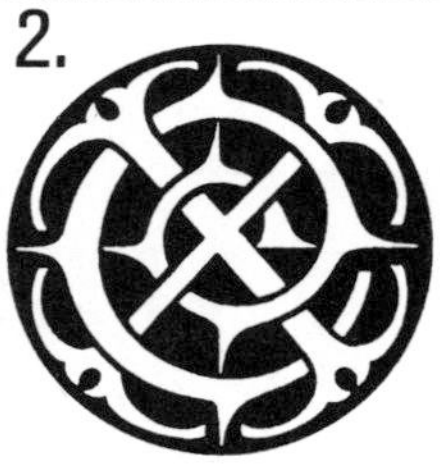

13.
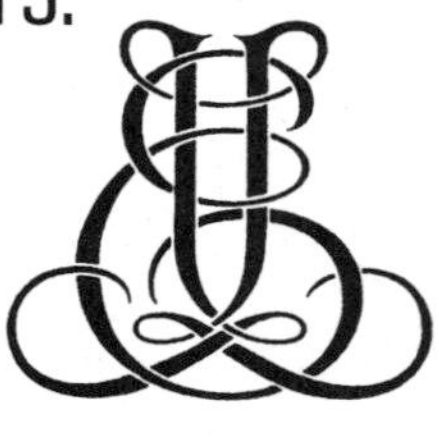

14.
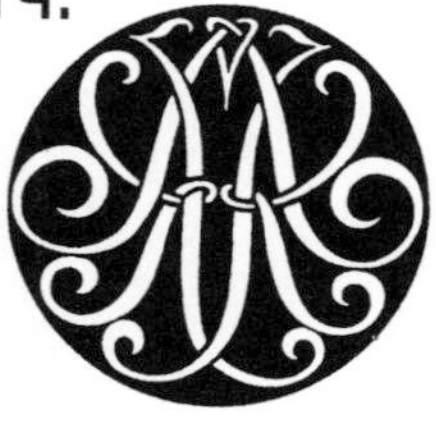

15.
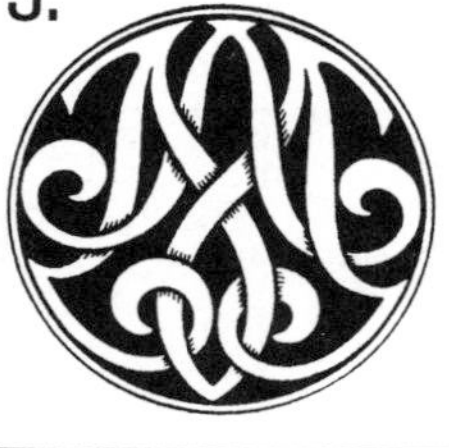

16.
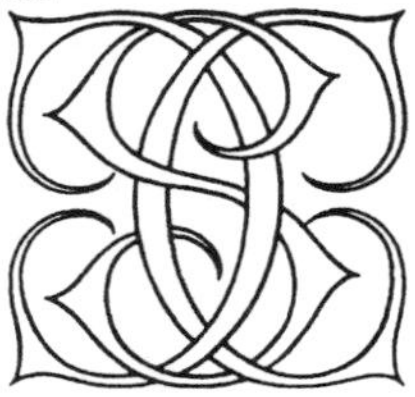

17.
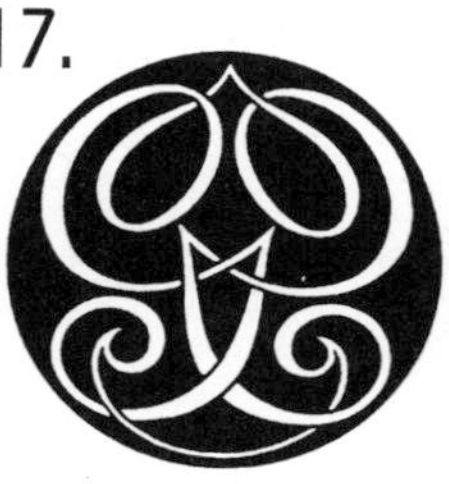

18.
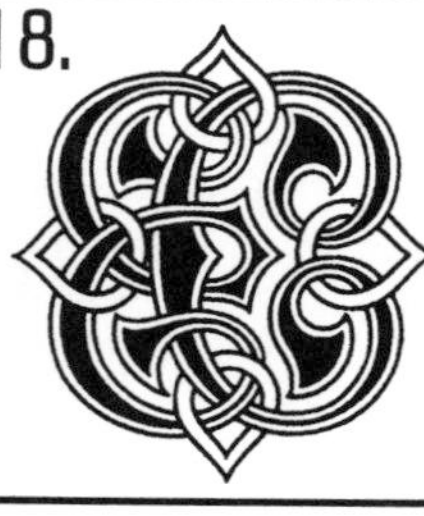

19.
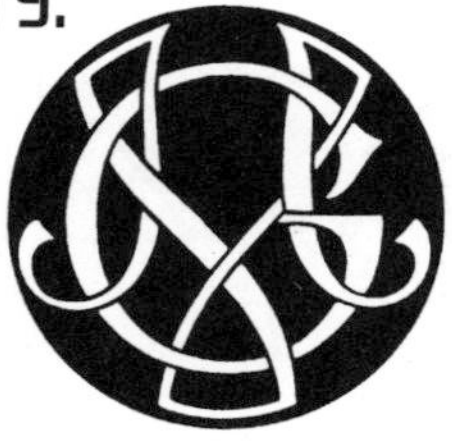

20.
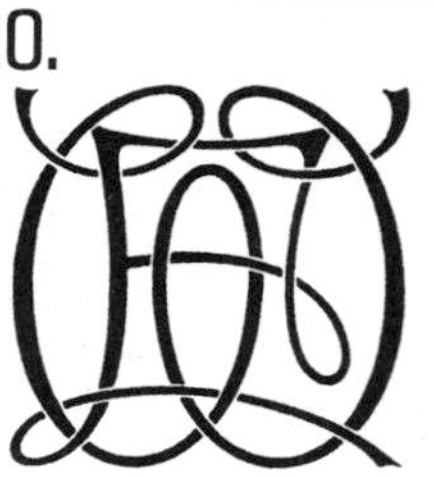

1. ________
2. ________
3. ________
4. ________

5. ________
6. ________
7. ________
8. ________

9. ________
10. ________
11. ________
12. ________

13. ________
14. ________
15. ________
16. ________

17. ________
18. ________
19. ________
20. ________

TARGET PRACTICE

Using each of the five numbers in the squares once, write a number sentence for each problem.

1. = (0)	7. = (6)
2. = (1)	8. = (7)
3. = (2)	9. = (8)
4. = (3)	10. = (9)
5. = (4)	11. = (10)
6. = (5)	12. = (11)

AN AMAZING PROPERTY OF TRIANGLES

In every triangle, the three

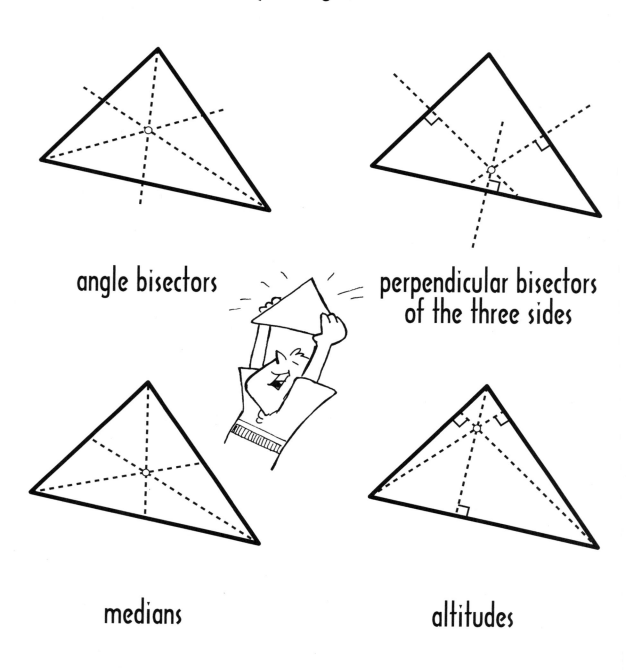

angle bisectors

perpendicular bisectors of the three sides

medians

altitudes

always meet at a common point.

WHEEL OF FRACTION

For each box, find the fractional part of a circle that corresponds with the fraction below the box. Place the letter of that fractional part in the box. What is the hidden message?

$\frac{3}{8}$ $\quad$ $\frac{1}{5}$ $\quad$ $\frac{5}{9}$ $\quad$ $\frac{2}{3}$ $\quad$ $\frac{1}{6}$ $\qquad$ $\frac{2}{7}$ $\quad$ $\frac{5}{9}$ $\quad$ $\frac{7}{8}$ $\quad$ $\frac{7}{8}$ $\quad$ $\frac{1}{4}$ $\quad$ $\frac{2}{5}$

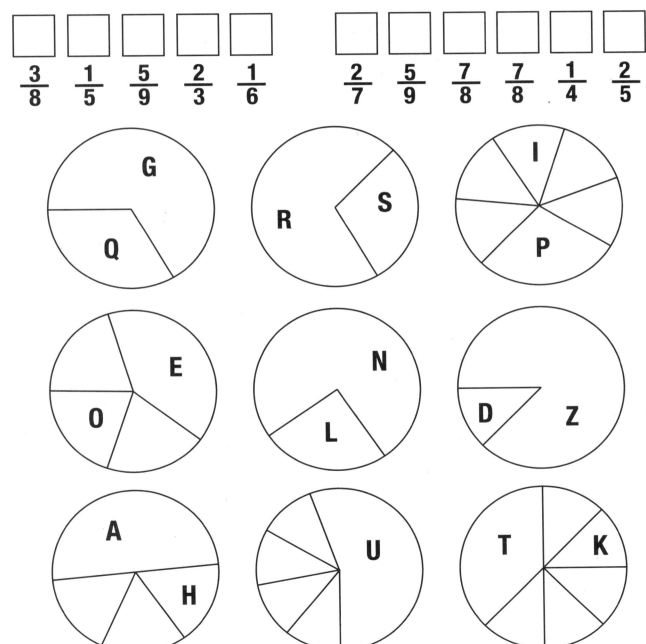

VISUAL THINKING

---

1. Which numbered shapes are congruent to which lettered shapes?

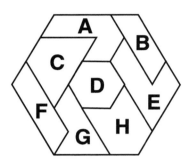   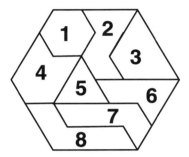

---

2. Sketch 3 circles:

   a. Divide one circle into 7 parts with 3 lines.
   b. Divide one circle into 6 parts with 3 lines.
   c. Divide one circle into 5 parts with 3 lines.

Note: The parts don't have to be the same size.

---

3. Find the point that is the same distance. . .

   a. from M and from R
   b. from R and from T
   c. from M and from S
   d. from R and from S

PROBLEMS TO SOLVE

1. Five hats are randomly distributed among the five people who own them. What is the probability that all of the people will receive their own hat?

2. What one shape fits all three holes exactly?

Source: *Thinking Visually: a Strategy Manual for Problem Solving* by Robert McKim, DSP, ISBN 0-86651-423-6.

3. What are the chances of drawing
   a. a red card from a regular 52-card deck of playing cards? ____
   b. a five? ____
   c. a black three? ____
   d. a spade? ____
   e. a seven of clubs? ____

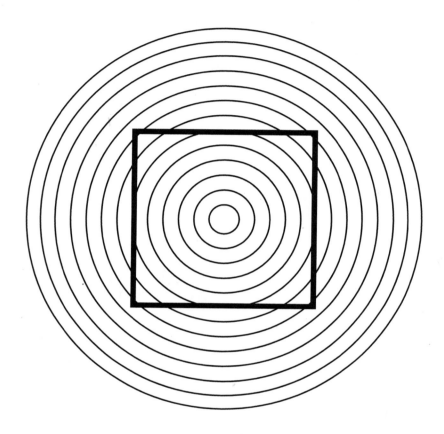

Is this a perfect square?

SYMMETRY

SYMMETRY
SYMMETRY

Complete each design by reflecting the image across the dotted vertical or horizontal line shown.

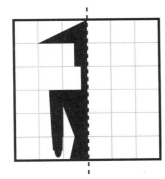
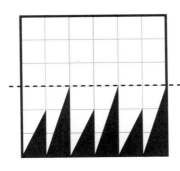
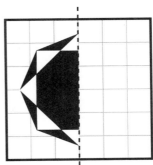

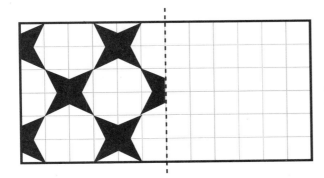
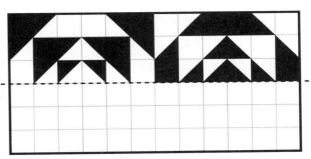

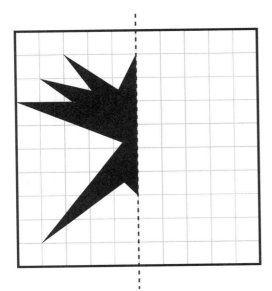
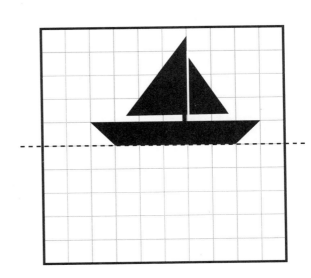

POLYIAMONDS

Polyiamonds are shapes made from equilateral triangles. Here are some polyiamond names:

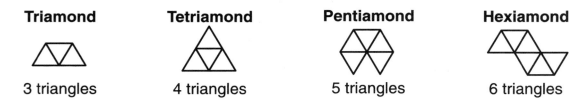

Triamond	Tetriamond	Pentiamond	Hexiamond
3 triangles	4 triangles	5 triangles	6 triangles

There are 12 different hexiamonds. Can you draw a different hexiamond on each of the grids provided? (The same shape turned a different direction is not different.) Optional: Give each of your shapes a fun name.

TARGET PRACTICE

Using each of the five numbers in the squares once, write a number sentence for each problem.

1. = **12**		7. = **18**	
2. = **13**		8. = **19**	
3. = **14**		9. = **20**	
4. = **15**		10. = **21**	
5. = **16**		11. = **22**	
6. = **17**		12. = **23**	

MAGIC SQUARE

A magic square is a square containing numbers in columns and rows. The sum of any row, any column, or any diagonal is the same. The sum in the magic square below is 15. This is a very difficult puzzle. Try it on your own if you like, but we have suggested a logical way to approach its solution below.

Suggested approach:

First: Make an organized list of possible combinations of 1 through 9 that total 15.

YOU FINISH IT!

DON'T USE THE SAME NUMBER TWICE IN A COMBINATION!

15

9 - 1 - 5
9 - 2 - 4
8 - 1 - 6
8 - 2 - ___

_____
_____
_____
_____

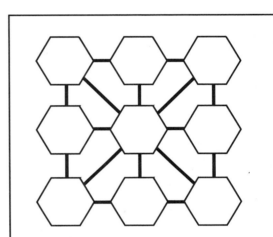

Place each of the digits 1 through 9 in the 9 hexagons so that the sum of each row, each column, and each diagonal is 15.

Second: Count how many different sums of 3 numbers that total 15 you will need in order to solve the problem. _____
How many sums does your list contain? _____

Third: Analyze the positions in the magic square. Each corner position fits in how many combinations? _____ Each middle side position? _____ The central position? _____

Finally: Use your list and position analysis to place numbers in logical positions and complete the puzzle. You have solved a difficult problem by using some organized listing and logical thinking.

QUADRILATERAL DISCOVERY

Sketch the four midpoints of each side of each of the quadrilaterals shown below. Then connect the midpoints of adjacent sides. What common pattern occurs with all the examples? What generalization could you make? Why is this true?

square	rectangle
parallelogram	rhombus
trapezoid	isosceles trapezoid
scalene quadrilateral	concave quadrilateral

PROBLEMS TO SOLVE

1. Using all four of the numbers 8, 4, 2 and 1, in that order, make equations that equal 0 through 10. (You may use the operations +, −, x and ÷ in any order and any number of times.) An equation that equals 6 is given as an example.

a. _____ = 0

b. _____ = 1

c. _____ = 2

d. _____ = 3

e. _____ = 4

f. _____ = 5

g. $\underline{\quad 8 - 4 + (2 \text{ x } 1) \quad}$ = 6

h. _____ = 7

i. _____ = 8

j. _____ = 9

k. _____ = 10

2. Five tangram puzzle pieces are shown below. Use the concepts of area and the Pythagorean Theorem to explain why the five pieces **will not** form a square.

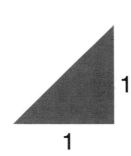

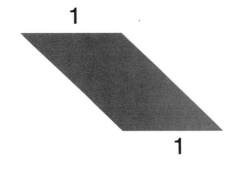

MATH DESIGNS

Here are some things you can do with the word "Math":

MATH **MATH** rotate it	**MATH** **MATH** **MATH** shrink it	**MATH** enlarge it	**HTAM MATH** reflect it
MATH reflect it	**MATH** sheer it	**MATH** outline it	**MATH** interrupt it
MATH smash it	**MATH** stretch it	**MATH** shadow it	**MATH** reverse it

Or you could:

Use geometric and graphic tools on a computer to play with your name.

ALPHA-NUMERIC PUZZLES

Alpha-numeric puzzles are computation problems written in letters instead of numerals. To make a solution, you'll need to figure out which numeral each letter represents. If a letter appears more than once, it represents the same number. One puzzle may have several different correct answers.

1.

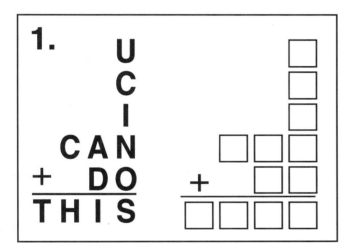

```
    U
    C
    I
  C A N
+   D O
T H I S
```

2.

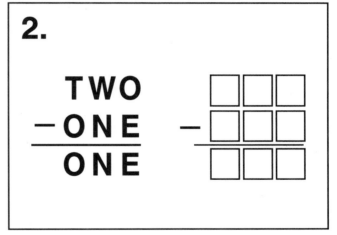

```
  T W O
− O N E
  O N E
```

3.

```
  O N E
  T W O
+ F I V E
E I G H T
```

4.

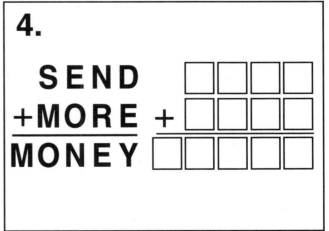

```
  S E N D
+ M O R E
M O N E Y
```

VISUAL THINKING

1. Which hexagons are divided into six congruent shapes?

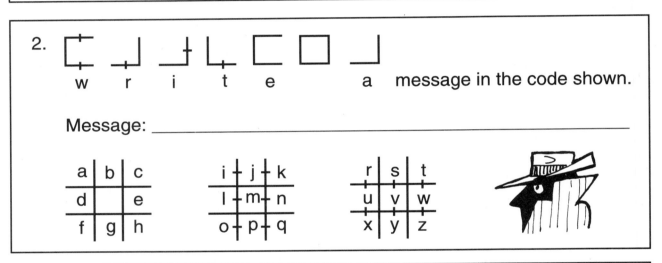

2.
```
┌┬  ┌  ┐  ┬┬  ┌  ┌─┐  ┐
│      │  │   │  │ │  │
```
w   r   i   t   e   a   message in the code shown.

Message: _____

a	b	c
d		e
f	g	h

i	j	k
l	m	n
o	p	q

r	s	t
u	v	w
x	y	z

3. These cubes are glued together. If one could lift the block of cubes and turn it around and upside down, how many cubes are not visible? _____

BOX FOLDING

Imagine that the pattern at the left of each problem is folded into a cube. Which of the four cubes would result? It may help to cut out your own pattern.

1.

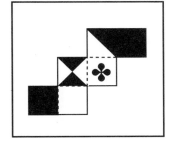

a.

b.

c.

d.

2.

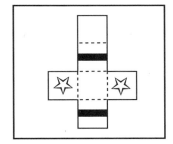

a.

b.

c.

d.

3.

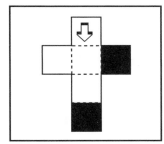

a.

b.

c.

d.

4.

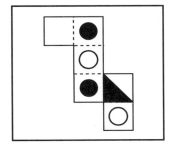

a.

b.

c.

d.

GEOMETRIC PATTERNS

TESSELLATING

Every parallelogram will **tessellate** the plane. You can get more interesting shapes by modifying the parallelograms. You can modify one side and then slide (translate) that change to the opposite side. The parallelogram no longer looks the same. It does, however, tessellate.

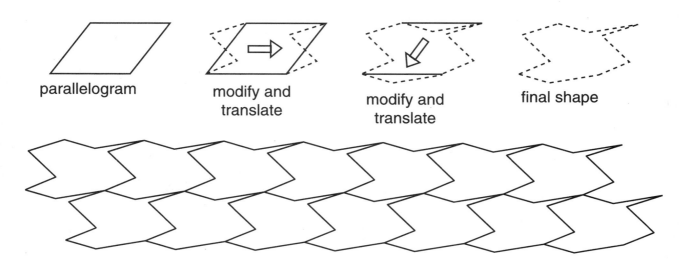

parallelogram

modify and
translate

modify and
translate

final shape

Try this technique of modifying the opposite sides of a parallelogram on the dot paper below. Then show that your shape tessellates.

HORSING AROUND

1. Last Friday at Eureka Fields Race Track:

   In the seventh race, with six horses racing, a strange thing happened.

   - The sum of the numbers of the two horses finishing first and last, second and fifth, and third and fourth was the same.

   - The sum of the numbers of the horses finishing first and the horse finishing next to last was 3 times the sum of the numbers of the horse finishing fourth and the horse finishing last.

   - The winning horse had an odd number.

   Give the order of the finish for the race.

1st	2nd	3rd	4th	5th	6th

2. An astute student in the audience recognized an unusual occurrence. The jockey of the winning horse weighed less than 100 pounds. Neither digit of his weight was an even number. The two digits were different. Their sum was greater than 7, and the weight was divisible by 7. Oh yes, the weight was not 1 greater or less than a square number.

   What was the jockey's weight? _____

TARGET PRACTICE

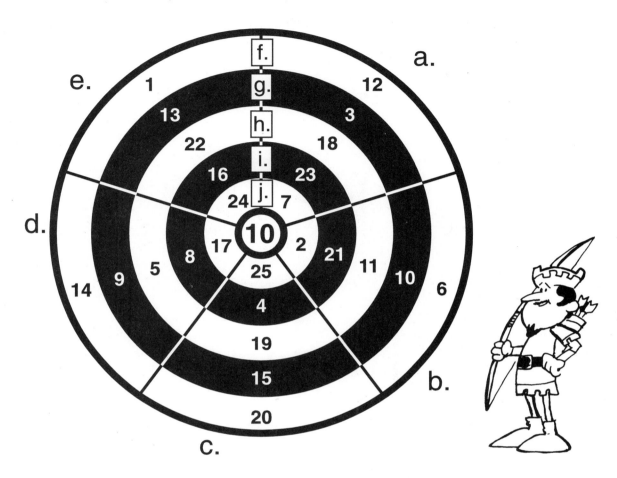

Use the numbers in the corresponding sector of each of the five rings to form a number sentence that equals the target value, 10.

a.	= 10
b.	= 10
c.	= 10
d.	= 10
e.	= 10

Use all of the numbers in one ring to form a number sentence that equals the target value, 10.

f.	= 10
g.	= 10
h.	= 10
i.	= 10
j.	= 10

HEXA (PARTIALLY) GON

Using the hexagon in the box with diagonals drawn, determine what fraction of each hexagon is black. Write your answer as a fraction in lowest terms.

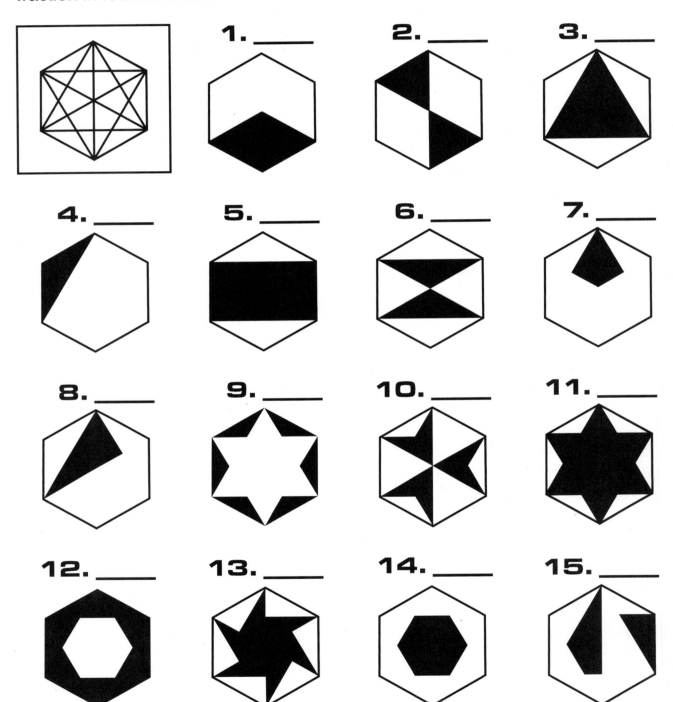

WHAT'S MY ANGLE?

You can measure angles with a protractor. You can also find angle measures by logical thinking. On these problems, don't use a protractor. Instead, remember that the sum of the three angles of any triangle is always 180˚, and the sum of the angles of any quadrilateral is always 360˚. Equilateral triangles are equiangular. Base angles of an isosceles triangle are congruent.

1. Given two squares and one equilateral triangle, find the measure of angle f. _____

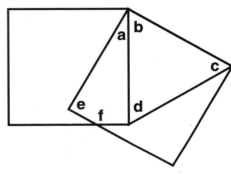

2. Find the measure of angle BCE. _____

3. Given triangle LMK is isosceles, find the measure of angle HGI. _____

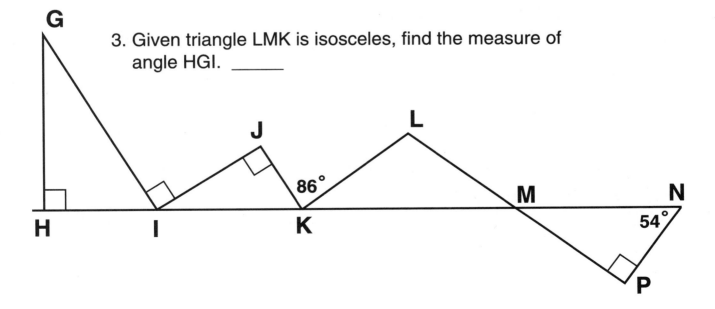

PASCAL'S TRIANGLE

This useful triangle has many practical applications. The triangle continues infinitely.

Pascal's Triangle contains many patterns. What patterns can you find?

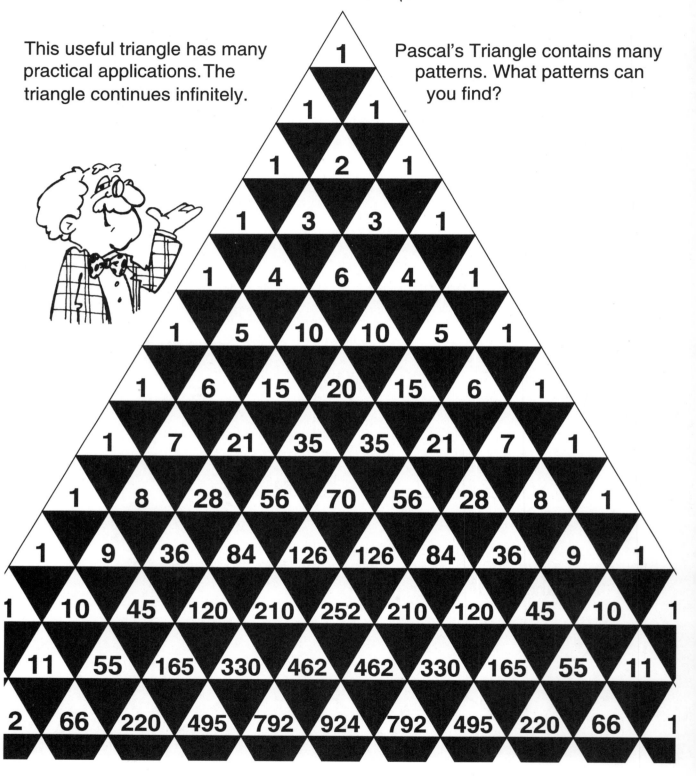

Combinations & Pascal's Triangle

Pascal's Triangle shows the combinations of things. Combination means the way things can be arranged when **the order of those things is not important**.

The fourth row of Pascal's Triangle represents the 16 combinations that 4 items can have. For instance, four girls are members of a photography club. The 16 possible arrangements of attendance at the club meeting are shown in the figure.

Pascal's Triangle

```
            1
          1   1
        1   2   1
      1   3   3   1
    1   4   6   4   1
  1   5  10  10   5   1
```

1	4	6	4	1
0 club members	1 club member	2 club members	3 club members	4 club members

Combinations & Pascal's Triangle

Pascal's Triangle shows the combinations of things. Combination means the way things can be arranged when **the order of those things is not important**. The fifth row in the triangle shows the number of different ways that five objects can be arranged. Complete the listing of different arrangements, using the five letters A through E as objects.

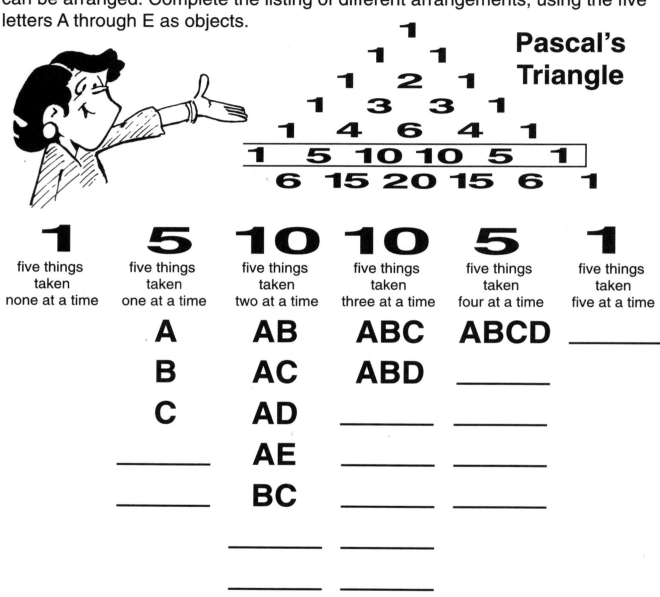

Pascal's Triangle

```
              1
            1   1
          1   2   1
        1   3   3   1
      1   4   6   4   1
    1   5   10  10  5   1
  6   15  20  15  6   1
```

1	**5**	**10**	**10**	**5**	**1**
five things taken none at a time	five things taken one at a time	five things taken two at a time	five things taken three at a time	five things taken four at a time	five things taken five at a time
	A	AB	ABC	ABCD	_____
	B	AC	ABD	_____	
	C	AD	_____	_____	
	_____	AE	_____	_____	
	_____	BC	_____	_____	
		_____	_____		
		_____	_____		
		_____	_____		
		_____	_____		
		_____			

Combinations & Permutations

Combinations and permutations are ways of counting or listing the arrangement of objects. They are very useful in several applications of mathematics such as phone numbers, license plates, medical research, lotteries, etc. When listing **combinations** of things, **order is not considered**. When listing **permutations** of things, **order is important**.

Combinations

five things taken
one at a time

A
B
C
D
E

five things taken
two at a time

AB
AC
AD
AE
BC
BD
BE
CD
CE
DE

five things taken
three at a time

ABC
ABD
ABE
ACD
ACE
ADE
BCD
BCE
BDE
CDE

five things taken
four at a time

ABCD
ABCE
ABDE
ACDE
BCDE

five things taken
five at a time

ABCDE

Pascal's Triangle

Permutations

five things taken
one at a time

A
B
C
D
E

five things taken
two at a time

AB	BA
AC	CA
AD	DA
AE	EA
BC	CB
BD	DB
BE	EB
CD	DC
DE	ED

five things taken
three at a time

ABC	ACB	BAC	BCA	CAB	CBA
ABD	ADB	BAD	BDA	DAB	DBA
ABE	AEB	BAE	BEA	EAB	EBA
ACD	ADC	CAD	CDA	DAC	DCA
ACE	AEC	CAE	CEA	EAC	ECA
ADE	AED	DAE	DEA	EAD	EDA
BCD	BDC	CBD	CDB	DBC	DCB
BCE	BEC	CBE	CEB	EBC	ECB
BDE	BED	DBE	DEB	EBD	EDB
CDE	CED	DCE	DEC	ECD	EDC

There are 120 permutations of five things taken four at a time. On another paper, **start** an organized listing of these permutations. List **at least 20** of the four-letter permutations.

MULTIPLES IN PASCAL'S TRIANGLE

Multiples of 2 are black hexagons.

Multiples of 3 are black hexagons.

Besides being interesting patterns themselves, these patterns enable us to guess what other prime multiple patterns in Pascal's Triangle would look like.

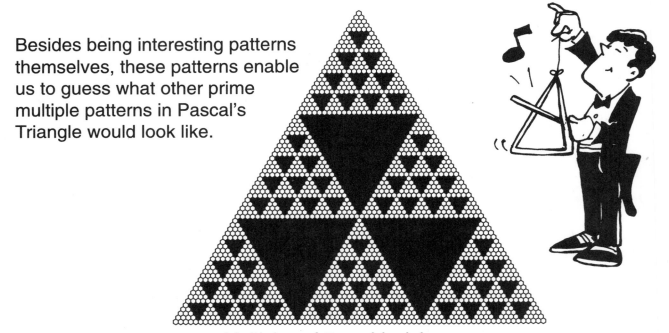

Multiples of 5 are black hexagons.

MATHEMATICS IS THE STUDY OF PATTERN

SIERPINSKI'S TRIANGLE

The pattern of triangles shown below is known as Sierpinski's Triangle. Five stages of the growth pattern are shown.

What fraction of each design is black?

1. _____   2. _____   3. _____   4. _____   5. _____

6. Do you see a pattern in the fractions? What fraction of the nth triangle would be black? _____

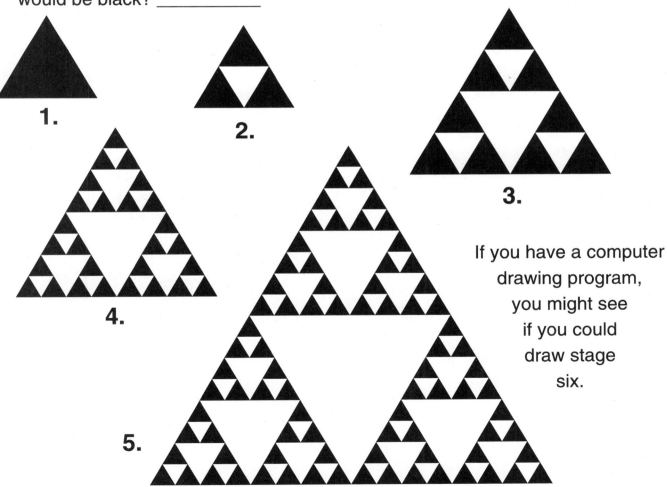

If you have a computer drawing program, you might see if you could draw stage six.

MOIRÉ PATTERNS

ONE SLICE OF A CUBE

It is possible to slice a cube with one straight cut (a plane) to result in a cross-section of the cube whose face has various geometric shapes. Sketch your sliced solution to each of the problems below:

Example: A square

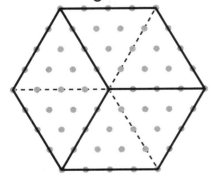

1. A rectangle that is not a square

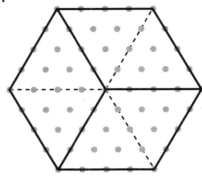

2. An equilateral triangle

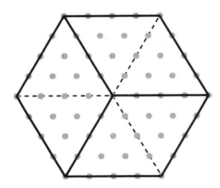

3. An isosceles triangle that is not equilateral

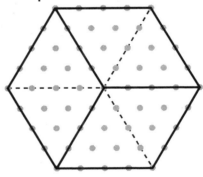

4. A scalene triangle

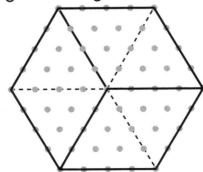

5. A regular hexagon

Ephesus, Turkey

Pearl Mosque, Delhi, India

Mexico City, Mexico

Beijing, China

Hangzhou, China

Western Expansion Memorial Arch, St. Louis, Missouri

All photos except lower right: Christine Freeman
Lower right photo: Dale Seymour

HOW MANY SQUARES?

Problem: How many different squares are in the figure at the right?

_____ squares

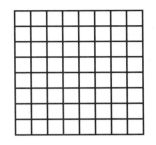

The problem above is a tough one because there are squares of many sizes. Searching for patterns is a very helpful technique in problems like this. Let's see how Margo approached the problem.

If figure had been...	Small sqs	2x2 sqs	3x3 sqs	4x4 sqs	5x5 sqs	Pattern	Ans.
□	□ 1					1	**1**
⊞	□ 4	□ 1				1 + 4	**5**
⊞	□ 9	□ 4	□ 1			1 + 4 + 9	**14**
⊞	□ 16	□ 9	□ 4	□ 1		1 + 4 + 9 + 16	**30**
⊞	□ 25	□ 16	□ 9	□ 4	□ 1	1 + 4 + 9 + 16 + 25	**55**
6 x 6	___	___	___	___	___	___	___
7 x 7	___	___	___	___	___	___	___
8 x 8	___	___	___	___	___	___	___
10 x 10	___	___	___	___	___	___	___
n x n	___	___	___	___	___	___	___

Study the chart. Find the patterns and fill in the blanks.

BELIEVE IT OR NOT

All powers of positive integers can be extracted from the sequence of consecutive odd numbers.

1. Complete the missing sequences in the chart below.

Power	Sequence of Consecutive Odd Numbers
2	$\underbrace{1}_{1^2}$ $\underbrace{1+3}_{2^2}$ $\underbrace{1+3+5}_{3^2}$ $\underbrace{1+3+5+7}_{4^2}$ $\underbrace{1+3+5+7+9}_{5^2}$ $\underbrace{1+3+5+7+9+11}_{6^2}$ $\ldots$
3	$\underbrace{1}_{1^3}$ $\underbrace{3+5}_{2^3}$ $\underbrace{7+9+11}_{3^3}$ $\underbrace{13+15+17+19}_{4^3}$ $\underbrace{21+23+25+27+29}_{5^3}$ $\ldots$
4	$\underbrace{}_{1^4}$ $\underbrace{}_{2^4}$ $\underbrace{}_{3^4}$ $\underbrace{}_{4^4}$
5	$\underbrace{}_{1^5}$ $\underbrace{15+17}_{2^5}$ $\underbrace{79+81+83}_{3^5}$ $\underbrace{253+255+257+259}_{4^5}$
6	$\underbrace{}_{1^6}$ $\underbrace{}_{2^6}$ $\underbrace{}_{3^6}$

2. A **perfect number** is a composite number that is equal to the sum of its divisors, excluding itself. The first five perfect numbers are given below. Write the first three as the sum of their divisors (excluding the number itself).

1st perfect number: 6 = <u>1</u> +__+__ 2nd perfect number: 28 = _____

3rd perfect number: 496 = _____

4th perfect number: 8,128 = _____

5th perfect number: 33,550,336 = _____

_____

Resources

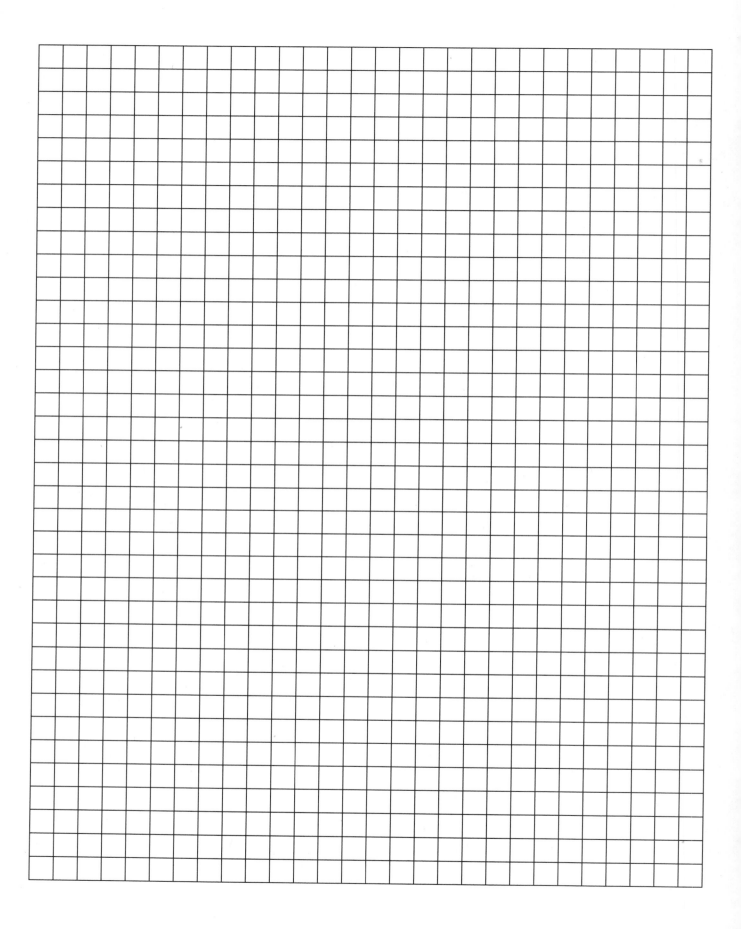

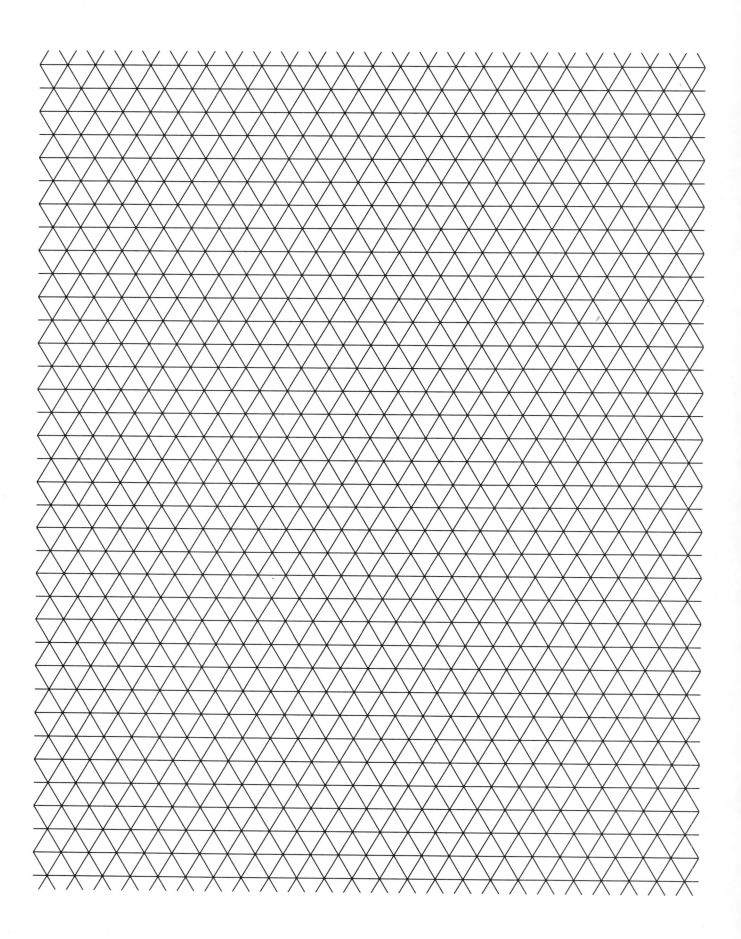

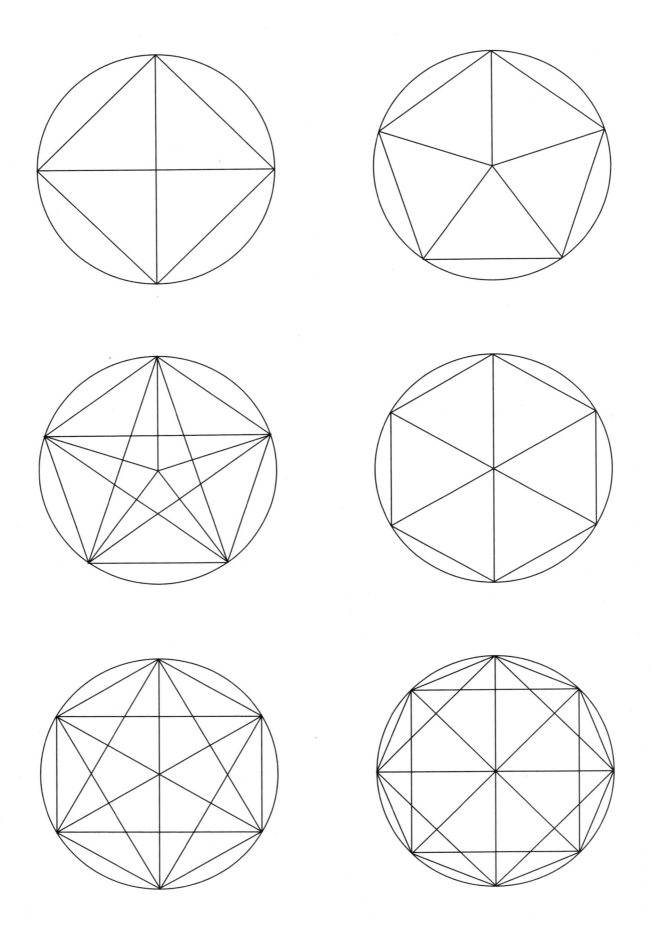

Smart Answers

1 One-Track Mind
1. C won the race.
2. Horses finished in this order: D B F A C E

3 Target Practice
Answers will vary but may include:

1. $12 \div (9 \div 3) = 4$
2. $12 + (9 \div 3) = 15$
3. $9 - (12 \div 3) = 5$
4. $(12 \div 3) \times 9 = 36$
5. $12 - (14 \div 2) = 5$
6. $(14 - 12) \div 2 = 1$
7. $14 + (12 \div 2) = 20$
8. $(12 \times 2) - 14 = 10$

4 Creating Number Patterns

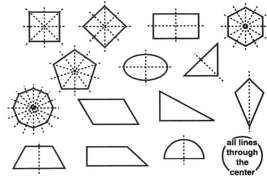

rule	n = 1	n = 2	n = 3	n = 4	n = 5	n = 6	n = 7
1. $n + 3$	4	5	6	7	8	9	10
2. $2n - 1$	1	3	5	7	9	11	13
3. $5n$	5	10	15	20	25	30	35
4. $3n + 2$	5	8	11	14	17	20	23
5. $3n^2$	9	36	81	144	225	324	441
6. n^3	1	8	27	64	125	216	343
7. $\frac{2n-1}{2}$	.5	1.5	2.5	3.5	4.5	5.5	6.5
8. $\frac{n(n+1)}{2}$	1	3	6	10	15	21	28

5 Lines of Symmetry

All *lines of symmetry*:

all lines through the center

8 Which One Differs?
1. c
2. f
3. d
4. e
5. f
6. c

9 Tangram Puzzle

12 Box Unfolding
1. d
2. d
3. c
4. c

13 Matchstick Puzzles

1.

2.

It's a tetrahedron, a three-dimensional pyramid

3.

15 Patchwork Fractions
1. $\frac{5}{9}$
2. $\frac{1}{2}$
3. $\frac{5}{9}$
4. $\frac{5}{9}$
5. $\frac{11}{25}$

17 Divide
Answers will vary but may include:

4 parts	5 parts	6 parts
7 parts	3 parts	2 parts
5 parts	6 parts	7 parts
8 parts	9 parts	10 parts

segments	1	2	3	4	5	n
parts	2	4	7	11	16	$\frac{n(n + 1) + 1}{2}$

22 Which Post is Tallest?
The three posts are the same length.

23 Target Practice
Answers will vary but may include:

1. $(6 - 4) \times (7 - 2) = 10$
2. $(5 \times 6) \div (3 \times 2) = 5$
3. $(6 \times 5) - (3 + 2) = 25$
4. $(6 \div 3) \times (2 \times 5) = 20$

24 Polyomino Puzzle

25 Cross Number Challenge

29 Sum Shapes

Answers may vary.

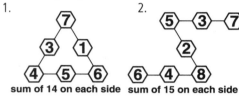

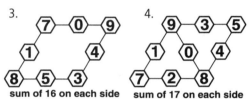

31 Who Am I?

1. 990   2. 20   3. 361   4. 174   5. 807

32 Box Unfolding

1. c   2. c   3. c   4. d

33 Hidden Shapes

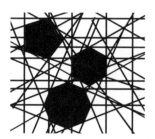

35 Tic-Tac-Number

36 Symmetry

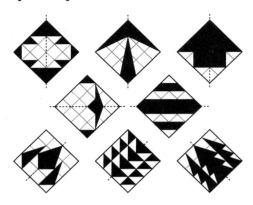

37 Problems to Solve

1.
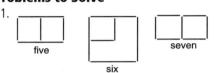

2. The trick is to divide the coins into three stacks before each weighing. Place two of the three stacks on the balance scale. If they balance, the light coin is in the third stack. If not, take the lighter third and repeat the process. Continue this approach; by the fifth weighing, you will have three stacks of one coin each.

3. 20 degrees. (The angle between three and four on the clock is 30 degrees, but the hour hand has moved one-third of the way between three and four by the time the minute hand has reached four.)

40 Same Shapes

1. c & q, g & l, k & t   2. e & y, b & x, f & q

41 Target Practice

1. $12 \div 4 + 3 - 6 = 0$
2. $4 + 6 + 3 - 12 = 1$
3. $12 \div [3 \times (6 - 4)] = 2$
4. $4 - [3 - (12 \div 6)] = 3$
5. $4 \times [3 - (12 - 6)] = 4$
6. $(12 + 3) - (4 + 6) = 5$
7. $(4 + 6) - (12 \div 3) = 6$
8. $(12 - 3) - (6 - 4) = 7$
9. $[(12 - 6) \times 4] \div 3 = 8$
10. $4 + 3 + (12 \div 6) = 9$
11. $6 \times 3 - 12 + 4 = 10$
12. $(12 + 6) - (4 + 3) = 11$

44 Being Observant

Answers may vary but may include:
1. Multiples of three
2. Products of two consecutive digits
3. Concave polygons
4. Multiples of 12
5. Fibonacci numbers
6. Triangular numbers, or the sum of consecutive digits with the first digit as 1

45 Sum Shapes

Answers may vary.

1.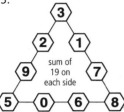

2.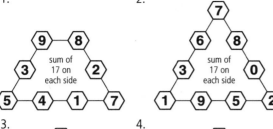

3.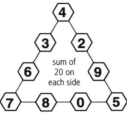

4.

47 Squares in Squares

1. Each is twice the area of the next smaller square.
2. One-fourth the area of the original square.
3. Larger by a factor of $\sqrt{2}$.
4. $n\sqrt{2}$.
5. Square #6

51 Fraction Puzzles

1.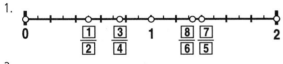

2.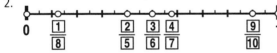

3.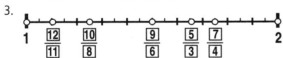

52 Visual Thinking

1. c, f, and g
2. a. I can read this.
   b. Run like the wind.
   c. Seeing is believing.
   d. Some letters look funny to me.
3. c

53 Target Practice

Answers may vary.
1. $10 \div (8 \div 4) - 5 = 0$
2. $(10 - 8) - (5 - 4) = 1$
3. $(5 \times 4) - (10 + 8) = 2$
4. $(10 - 8) + (5 - 4) = 3$
5. $(8 \div 4) + (10 \div 5) = 4$
6. $10 + [5 - (8 \div 4)] =$
7. $(8 - 4) + (10 - 8) = 6$
8. $(8 + 5) - (10 - 4) = 7$
9. $8 \div [10 - (5 + 4)] = 8$
10. $(10 + 8) - (5 + 4) = 9$
11. $10 \div [4 - (8 - 5)] = 10$
12. $(4 + 5) + (10 - 8) = 11$

55 Geometric Relationships

1. A polygon can be a quadrilateral.
2. A square is always a rectangle.
3. A parallelogram is always a quadrilateral.
4. A rhombus can be a square.
5. A rectangle is always a parallelogram.
6. A quadrilateral can be a rhombus.
7. A trapezoid is never a parallelogram.
8. A square is never a trapezoid.
9. A rectangle is always a quadrilateral.
10. A quadrilateral is always a polygon.
11. A rhombus can be a rectangle.
12. A square is always a parallelogram.
13. A parallelogram can be a rhombus.
14. A square is always a rhombus.
15. A rhombus is always a parallelogram.

56 Square & Hexagon Puzzle

57 Juggling Digits

1. 304, 313, 322, 331, 340, 403, 412, 421, 430, 502, 511, 520, 601, 610, and 700
2. 109, 127, 145, 163, 181, 217, 235, 253, 271, 307, 325, 343, 361, 415, 433, and 451
3. 506, 524, 542, 560, 614, 632, 650, 704, 722, 740, 812, 830, and 902.
4. 965

59 Digit Dilemmas

1. Digits: 4, 4 and 1. Square numbers: 144 and 441.
2. 10, 14, 15, and 21
3. One of their two digits is a one.
4. 99

60 Same Shapes

6 and 20; 17 and 24; 4 and 16; 7 and 15; 1 and 28.

61 Alpha-Numeric Puzzles

Answers may vary.

1.
```
  FOUR    5431
+ FOUR  + 5431
 EIGHT  10862
```

2.
```
 THREE    36255
+ FOUR  +  8902
 SEVEN   45157
```

3.
```
  ONE     217
  TWO     942
+ SIX   + 358
 NINE   1517
```

4.
```
  ADD     388
  FOR     457
+  DE  +   81
  SUM     926
```

63 Geo-Match

1. i	2. f	3. p	4. k
5. x	6. v	7. l	8. n
9. c	10. h	11. b	12. e
13. g	14. w	15. d	16. a
17. u	18. q	19. s	20. j

64 Symmetry in Design

What the designers had in mind:

1. OZ	2. GGN	3. LX	4. GGH
5. FFT	6. EE	7. TT	8. MMR
9. WWN	10. WWO	11. LLC	12. CX
13. LLE	14. KKA	15. AM	16. CCS
17. GG	18. EC	19. GM	20. FW

65 Target Practice

Answers may vary.

1. $(9 - 8) - [7 - (3 \times 2)] = 0$
2. $(9 - 8) \div [7 - (3 \times 2)] = 1$
3. $[(7 - 2) + (9 - 8)] = 2$
4. $[(7 - 2) + (9 - 8)] - 3 = 3$
5. $(8 \div 2) \times [3 - (9 - 7)] = 4$
6. $(8 - 3) + [9 - (7 + 2)] = 5$
7. $7 - [(8 \div 2) - (9 \div 3)] = 6$
8. $(9 + 2 + 7) - (8 + 3) = 7$
9. $7 + [(8 \div 2) - (9 \div 3)] = 8$
10. $(9 + 3 + 7) - (8 + 2) = 9$
11. $3 + 8 - [9 \div (2 + 7)] = 10$
12. $(3 + 8 + 9) - (2 + 7) = 11$

67 Wheel of Fraction

TOUGH PUZZLE

68 Visual Thinking

1. 1-D, 3-C, 4-H, and 6-G.
2. Answers may vary. (See figures).

3. a. T   b. S   c. A   d. N

69 Problems to Solve

1. $\frac{1}{120}$

2.

3. a. $\frac{1}{2}$ b. $\frac{1}{13}$ c. $\frac{1}{26}$

   d. $\frac{1}{4}$ e. $\frac{1}{52}$

70 Is This a Perfect Square?

Yes

71 Symmetry

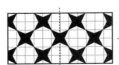 

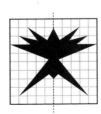 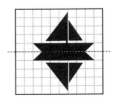

72 Polyiamonds

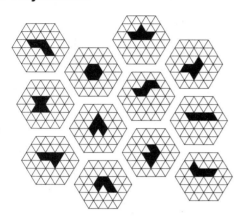

73 Target Practice

Answers may vary.

1. $[9 \div (21 \div 7)] + 5 + 4 = 12$
2. $9 + (21 \div 7) + (5 - 4) = 13$
3. $(21 - 9 - 7) + 5 + 4 = 14$
4. $(9 + 7) - [21 - (5 \times 4)] = 15$
5. $(9 + 7) \times [21 - (5 \times 4)] = 16$
6. $\{[9 \div (21 \div 7)] \times 4\} + 5 = 17$
7. $21 - (9 - 7) - (5 - 4) = 18$
8. $\{[9 \div (21 \div 7)] \times 5\} + 4 = 19$
9. $21 - [(9 - 7) - (5 - 4)] = 20$
10. $21 \times [(9 - 7) - (5 - 4)] = 21$
11. $21 + [(9 - 7) - (5 - 4)] = 22$
12. $[21 + (9 - 7)] \times (5 - 4) = 23$

75 Sum Shapes

Answers may vary.

1. $9 - 1 - 5$
   $9 - 2 - 4$
   $8 - 1 - 6$
   $8 - 2 - 5$
   $8 - 3 - 4$
   $7 - 2 - 6$
   $7 - 3 - 5$
   $6 - 4 - 5$
2. 8, 8
3. corner: 3   middle side: 2   central: 4
4.

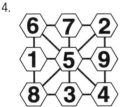

76 Quadrilateral Discovery

Answers will vary somewhat. Common pattern and generalization: Joining the four midpoints forms a parallelogram. If you draw one diagonal of any of the quadrilaterals, you have formed two triangles. Why true: A line joining the midpoints of two sides of a triangle is parallel to the third side and equal to one-half the third side. Lines parallel to the same line are parallel to each other. If opposite sides of a quadrilateral are parallel, the figure is a parallelogram.

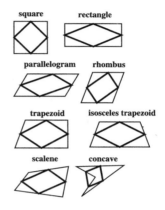

77 Problems to Solve

1. Answers may vary.
   a. $8 - (4 \times 2) \times 1 = 0$
   b. $8 - 4 - 2 - 1 = 1$
   c. $(8 - 4) - (2 \times 1) = 2$
   d. $(8 - 4) - 2 + 1 = 3$
   e. $(8 \div 4) + (2 \div 1) = 4$
   f. $(8 \div 4) + 2 + 1 = 5$
   g. $4 + (2 \times 1) = 6$
   h. $8 - 4 + 2 + 1 = 7$
   i. $8 \div (4 - 2 - 1) = 8$
   j. $8 + (4 - 2 - 1) = 9$
   k. $8 + 4 - (2 \times 1) = 10$

2. The areas of the five shapes combined would be $\frac{11}{2}$ square units (or $5\frac{1}{2}$ units). So, the required edge length of the square to be made would be $\sqrt{\frac{11}{2}}$. The lengths of the sides of the shapes are $\sqrt{1}$, $\sqrt{2}$, 2 and $2\sqrt{2}$. It is not possible to form a line $\sqrt{\frac{11}{2}}$ long with pieces having those lengths.

79 Alpha-Numeric Puzzles

Answers may vary.

1.
```
      U        7
      C        9
      I        3
    CAN      965
   +  DO    + 48
   THIS    1032
```

2.
```
   TWO    472
  -ONE   -236
   ONE    236
```

3.
```
    ONE     621
    TWO     846
  +FIVE   +9071
  EIGHT   10538
```

4.
```
   SEND     9567
  +MORE   +1085
  MONEY   10652
```

80 Visual Thinking

1. a, b, c, e, g, i, j

ᒣᒧᑌᐉᑕ ᒧᗢᗝᐉ ᒳᗗᗗᗝᑫ ᒧ ᒧ ᑎ

2. ("Answers will vary.")
3. 2 cubes

81 Box Folding

1. d   2. b   3. b   4. d

85 Horsing Around

1st	2nd	3rd	4th	5th	6th
5	3	6	1	4	2

2. Jockey's weight was 91 pounds.

87 Target Practice

Answers may vary.

a. $(17 - 7) \times [2 - (25 - 24)] = 10$
b. $4 \times (23 - 21) + (16 \div 8) = 10$
c. $5 \times (22 \div 11) \times (19 - 18) = 10$
d. $10 \times [(9 \div 3) - (15 - 13)] = 10$
e. $12 - 1 - [(20 - 14) \div 6] = 10$
f. $12 [(3 + 7) \div (23 - 18)] = 10$
g. $(21 - 11) \times [6 (10 \div 2)] = 10$
h. $[(25 + 15) \div 4] \times (20 - 19) = 10$
i. $17 - 8 + [(9 + 5) \div 14] = 10$
j. $(13 + 1) - [24 \div (22 - 16)] = 10$

88 Hexa(partially)gon

1. $\frac{1}{3}$ 2. $\frac{1}{3}$ 3. $\frac{1}{2}$

4. $\frac{1}{6}$ 5. $\frac{2}{3}$ 6. $\frac{1}{3}$ 7. $\frac{1}{6}$

8. $\frac{1}{4}$ 9. $\frac{1}{3}$ 10. $\frac{1}{3}$ 11. $\frac{2}{3}$

12. $\frac{2}{3}$ 13. $\frac{5}{12}$ 14. $\frac{1}{3}$ 15. $\frac{11}{36}$

89 What's My Angle?

1. 150°   2. 52°   3. 32°

90 Pascal's Triangle

Answers will vary, but, before any popular books were available on Pascal's Triangle, two eighth-grade girls in the author's class wrote a 72-page report on patterns they found in the triangle. Here are a few of the patterns they included: Any number is the sum of the two numbers above it; the sum of the numbers in any row is twice the sum of the number in the row above it; the sum of any row is a power of two; each row is a power of 11; and, diagonals include the counting numbers and the triangular numbers.

92 Combinations & Pascal's Triangle

A	AB	ABC	ABCD	ABCDE
B	AC	ABD	ABCE	
C	AD	ABE	ABDE	
D	AE	ACD	BCDE	
E	BC	ACE		
	BD	ADE		
	BE	BCD		
	CD	BCE		
	CE	BDE		
	DE	CDE		

93 Combinations & Permutations

List of *some* of the permutations of five things taken four at a time:

ABCD	ADBC	BACD	BDAC	CABD
ABCE	ADBE	BACE	BDAE	CABE
ABDC	ADCB	BADC	BDCA	
ABDE	ADCE	BADE	BDCE	
ABEC	ADEB	BAEC	BDEA	
ABED	ADEC	BAED	BDEC	
ACBD	AEBC	BCAD	BEAC	
ACBE	AEBD	BCAE	BEAD	
ACDB	AECB	BCDA	BECA	
ACDE	AECD	BCDE	BECD	
ACEB	AEDB	BCEA	BEDA	
ACED	AEDC	BCED	BEDC	

95 Sierpinski's Triangle

1. 1   2. $\frac{3}{4}$ 3. $\frac{9}{16}$ 4. $\frac{27}{64}$ 5. $\frac{81}{256}$

6. Pattern: numerator is a power of three; denominator is a power of four. The nth triangle would be $\frac{3^{(n-1)}}{4^{(n-1)}}$ black.

97 One Slice of a Cube

Example: A square

1. A rectangle that is not a square

2. An equilateral triangle

3. An isosceles triangle that is not equilateral

4. A scalene triangle

5. A regular hexagon

99 How Many Squares?

1. 204 squares altogether

2.

6×6	36	25	16	9	4	$1 + 4 + \ldots + 36$	91
7×7	49	36	25	16	9	$1 + 4 + \ldots + 49$	140
8×8	64	49	36	25	16	$1 + 4 + \ldots + 64$	204
9×9	81	64	49	36	25	$1 + 4 + \ldots + 81$	285
10×10	100	81	64	49	36	$1 + 4 + \ldots + 100$	385
$n \times n$	n	$(n - 1)^2$	$(n - 2)^2$	$(n - 3)^2$	$(n - 4)^2$	$1 + 4 + \ldots + n^2$	

100 Believe It or Not

1. $1^4 = 1$
   $2^4 = 7 + 9$
   $3^4 = 25 + 27 + 29$
   $4^4 = 61 + 63 + 65 + 67$
   $1^5 = 1$
   $1^6 = 1$
   $2^6 = 31 + 33$
   $3^6 = 241 + 243 + 245$

2. $6 = 1 + 2 + 3$
   $28 = 1 + 2 + 4 + 7 + 14$
   $496 = 1 + 2 + 4 + 8 + 16 + 31 + 62 + 124 + 248$

More Smart Books

Locate the puzzle, activity, or challenge that interests you. Then match the corresponding numbers in "Smart Books to Check" with the numbered books on the facing page.

Page	Puzzles, Challenges, and Activities	Smart Books to Check (see page 119)
1	One-Track Mind	49, 54
2	Star Designs	2, 33
3	Target Practice	46
5	Lines of Symmetry	27, 50
6	Geometric Patterns	42
7	Drawing Patterns	42
8	Which One Differs?	34
9	Tangram Puzzle	23, 45
10	Visual: Ellipse Chords	39
11	Straight-Line Curves	41, 43
12	Box Unfolding	48
13	Matchstick Puzzles	7
14	Modern Star	9
15	Patchwork Fractions	9
16	Impossible Tri-Bar	13
17	Divide	38
20	Star Designs	35, 39
21	Star Designs	35, 39
22	Which Post is Tallest?	5, 51
23	Target Practice	46
24	Polyomino Puzzle	11, 16, 23
25	Cross Number Challenge	3, 8, 40
26	Kaleidoscope Designs	15, 19
27	Kaleidoscope Design	14, 19
28	Visual: Checkboard Illusion	5, 51
29	Sum Shapes	44
30	Drawing Patterns	42
31	Who Am I?	40

Page	Puzzles, Challenges, and Activities	Smart Books to Check (see page 119)
32	Box Unfolding	48
35	Tic-Tac-Number	3, 8
36	Symmetry	22
37	Problems to Solve	15, 38
38	Star Designs	2, 39
39	Creating a Design	35, 39
41	Target Practice	46
42	Islamic Designs	12, 39
43	Islamic Designs	12, 39
44	Being Observant	3, 34
45	Sum Shapes	44
47	Squares in Squares	15, 38
48	Basic Geometric Constructions	35, 39
49	Can You Construct…?	35, 39
50	Constructing Regular Pentagon	35, 39
52	Visual Thinking	48
53	Target Practice	46
54	Visual: Inscribed Hexagons	41
56	Square & Hexagon Puzzle	23
57	Juggling Digits	38
59	Digit Dilemmas	40
61	Alpha-Numeric Puzzles	6
62	Geometric Patterns	42
65	Target Practice	46
66	An Amazing Property	35, 39
68	Visual Thinking	48
69	Problems to Solve	24, 38

Page	Puzzles, Challenges, and Activities	Smart Books to Check (see page 119)
70	Is This a Perfect Square?	5, 51
71	Symmetry	22
72	Polyiamonds	16
73	Target Practice	46
74	Visual: Line Design	41, 43
75	Magic Squares	25, 38
77	Problems To Solve	45, 46
79	Alpha-Numeric Puzzles	6
80	Visual Thinking	48
81	Box Folding	48
82	Geometric Patterns	42
83	Tessellating	42
85	Horsing Around	54
86	Visual: Line Design	41, 43
87	Target Practice	46
90	Pascal's Triangle	18, 47
91	Combinations & Pascal's Triangle	18, 47
92	Combinations & Pascal's Triangle	18, 47
93	Combinations & Permutations	18, 47
94	Multiples in Pascal's Triangle	47
95	Sierpinski's Triangle	47
96	Moiré Patterns	17
97	One Slice of a Cube	24
98	Photo: Arcs & Arches	4, 28
99	How Many Squares?	38
100	Believe It or Not	3

1. Agostini, Franco. *Math and Logic Games.* New York: Harper and Row, 1983.

2. Beard, Col. Robert S. *Patterns In Space.* Chicago: Creative Publications, 1973.

3. Bezuska, Stanley, and Margaret Kenney. *Number Treasury.* White Plains, NY: Dale Seymour Publications, 1982.

4. Blackwell, William. *Geometry in Architecture.* Berkeley, CA: Key Curriculum Press, 1984.

5. Block, J. R., and H. E. Yuker. *Can You Believe Your Eyes?* New York: Gardner Press, 1989.

6. Brooke, Maxey. *150 Puzzles in Crypt-Arithmetic.* New York: Dover Publications, 1969.

7. Brooke, Maxey. Tricks, *Games and Puzzles With Matches.* New York: Dover Publications, 1973.

8. Clark, Dave. *More Tic-Tac-Toe Math.* White Plains, NY: Dale Seymour Publications, 1996.

9. Cohen, Luanne Seymour. *Quilt Design Masters.* White Plains, NY: Dale Seymour Publications, 1996.

10. Davidson, Patricia, and Robert Willcut. *Spatial Problem Solving.* White Plains, NY: Cuisenaire Co. of America, 1984.

11. Duby, Marjorie. *Try It! Pentaminoes.* White Plains, NY: Cuisenaire Co. of America, 1992.

12. El-Said, Issam, and Ayse Parman. *Geometric Concepts in Islamic Art.* White Plains, NY: Dale Seymour Publications, 1976.

13. Ernst, Bruno. *Adventures With Impossible Figures.* Norfolk, England: Tarquin Publications, 1987.

14. Finkel, Norma Yvette, and Leslie Finkel. *Kaleidoscope Designs and How to Create Them.* New York: Dover Publications, 1980.

15. Fisher, Lyle. *Super Problems.* White Plains, NY: Dale Seymour Publications, 1982.

16. Golomb, Solomon. *Polyominoes,* Rev. Ed. Princeton, NJ: Princeton University Press, 1994.

17. Grafton, Carol Belanger. *Optical Designs in Motion With Moiré Overlays.* New York: Dover Publications, 1976.

18. Green, Thomas, and Charles Hamburg. *Pascal's Triangle.* White Plains, NY: Dale Seymour Publications, 1986.

19. Kennedy, Joe, and Diane Thomas. *Kaleidoscope Math.* Chicago; Creative Publications, 1978.

20. Kenneway, Eric. *Complete Origami.* New York: St Martin's Press, 1987.

21. Kremer, Ron. *Exploring With Squares and Cubes.* White Plains, NY: Dale Seymour Publications, 1989.

22. Kroner, Louis R. *Slides, Flips and Turns.* White Plains, NY: Dale Seymour Publications, 1984.

23. Lindgren, Harry. *Recreational Problems In Geometric Dissections.* New York: Dover Publications, 1972.

24. McKim, Robert. *Thinking Visually.* White Plains, NY: Dale Seymour Publications, 1997.

25. Moran, Jim. *The Wonders of Magic Squares.* New York: Vintage Books, 1982.

26. Murray, William, and Francis Rigney. *Paper Folding For Beginners.* New York: Dover Publications, 1960.

27. Neale, Robert, and Thomas Hull. *Origami, Plain and Simple.* New York: St Martin's Press, 1994.

28. Norwich, John Julius, ed., et al. *Great Architecture of the World.* New York: Da Capo Press, 1991.

29. Pearce, Peter, and Susan Pearce. *Polyhedra Primer.* White Plains, NY: Dale Seymour Publications, 1978.

30. Picciotto, Henri. *Pentamino Activities, Lessons and Puzzles.* Chicago: Creative Publications, 1986.

31. Pollard, Jeanne. *Building Toothpick Bridges.* White Plains, NY: Dale Seymour Publications, 1985.

32. Rozell, Paula. *Plotting Pictures;* Grades 5–8. White Plains, NY: Dale Seymour Publications, 1997.

33. Runion, Garth. *The Golden Section.* White Plains, NY: Dale Seymour Publications, 1990.

34. Seymour, Dale, Mary Laycock, Ruth Heller and Bob Larsen. *Aftermath* (Series). Chicago: Creative Publications, 1970.

35. Seymour, Dale, and Schadler Reuben. *Creative Constructions,* Rev. Ed. Chicago: Creative Publications, 1974.

36. Seymour, Dale, and Ed Beardslee. *Critical Thinking Activities* (Series). White Plains: Dale Seymour Publications, 1988.

37. Seymour, Dale, and Richard Gidley. *Eureka,* Rev. Ed. Chicago: Creative Publications, 1972.

38. Seymour, Dale. *Favorite Problems.* White Plains, NY: Dale Seymour Publications, 1982.

39. Seymour, Dale. *Geometric Design.* White Plains, NY: Dale Seymour Publications, 1988.

40. Seymour, Dale, and John Gregory. *I'm a Number Game.* Chicago: Creative Publications, 1978.

41. Seymour, Dale. *Introduction to Line Designs.* White Plains, NY: Dale Seymour Publications, 1992.

42. Seymour, Dale, and Jill Britton. *Introduction to Tessellations.* White Plains, NY: Dale Seymour Publications, 1989.

43. Seymour, Dale, Linda Silvey and Joyce Snider. *Line Designs,* Rev. Ed. Chicago: Creative Publications, 1974.

44. Seymour, Dale. *Sum Puzzles.* Chicago: Creative Publications, 1979.

45. Seymour, Dale. *Tangramath.* Chicago: Creative Publications, 1971.

46. Seymour, Dale, and Margo Seymour. *Target Practice* (Series). White Plains, NY: Dale Seymour Publications, 1993.

47. Seymour, Dale. *Visual Patterns in Pascal's Triangle.* White Plains, NY: Dale Seymour Publications, 1986.

48. Seymour, Dale. *Visual Thinking Cards* (Series). White Plains, NY: Dale Seymour Publications, 1983.

49. Sherard, Wade H. III, *Logic Number Problems.* White Plains, NY: Dale Seymour Publications, 1997.

50. Silvey, Linda, and Loretta Taylor. *Paper and Scissors Polygons and More.* White Plains, NY: Dale Seymour Publications, 1997.

51. Simon, Seymour. *The Optical Illusions Book.* New York: Beech Tree Books, 1976.

52. Spangenburg, Ray, and Diane K. Moser. *The Story of American Bridges (Connecting a Continent Series).* New York: Facts on File, 1991 (out of print).

53. Wilkinson, Philip, and Paolo Donati (illustrator). *Amazing Buildings.* London: DK Publishing, 1993.

54. Williams, Wayne. *Quizzles.* White Plains, NY: Dale Seymour Publications, 1997.

Smart Math Web Sites

In the time it takes to publish this book, a list of Web sites could easily become a bit out of date. With that caveat, here are sites that offer more mathematical puzzles, challenges, and beautiful images. If you find a site no longer available, try links from another site to newer sites on related topics. Explore!

Bullpup Math Resources. A middle-school site with toothpick (matchstick) puzzles, problem-of-the-day offerings, links to online math-problem contests, and links to online puzzle "rings" (strings of Web sites).
http://www.siue.edu/~jbasden/math.htm

Enchanted Mind. Visual and logic puzzles, such as tangrams, pentominos, pyramids; variety from National Center for Creativity. Online and printable puzzles.
http://enchantedmind.com/puzzle.htm

Fibonacci and the Golden Section. Explanations, a page of easier Fibonacci puzzles, and applications in art, architecture, and music.
http://www.ee.surrey.ac.uk/Personal/R.Knott/Fibonacci/fib.html

Geometry Through Art.
http://forum.swarthmore.edu/~sarah/shapiro/

Interactive Mathematics Miscellany and Puzzles. Online and printable puzzles and games, fun even for those who "hate" math; also available on CD-ROM.
http://www.cut-the-knot.com/

Magic Squares. Unit for upper elementary and middle-school students.
http://forum.swarthmore.edu/alejandre/magic.square.html

Math Forum (Swarthmore College). Showcases great activities on specific math concepts, such as dividing by zero, magic squares, polyhedra, Pascal's triangle, making tesselations, famous math problems. Links to many math problems and puzzles on the Internet.
http://forum.swarthmore.edu/.

Mathematical Problem Solving Task Centres. Monthly mathematically-oriented problem for various grade levels, with past problems cataloged. From Mathematical Association of Victoria, Australia.
http://www.srl.rmit.edu.au/mav/PSTC/general/index.html

Pascal's Triangle. Lessons and worksheets.
http://forum.swarthmore.edu/workshops/usi/pascal/pascal_lessons.html#lessons

Perspective Drawing, Moebius Strip, Polyhedra, and Spreadsheets.
http://forum.swarthmore.edu/sum95/math_and/

Symbolic Sculpture and Mathematics. Gallery of mathematical sculptures by John Robinson (such as on page 34). Math explanations and construction tips on structures such as rings, bands, knots, and fractals.
http://www.bangor.ac.uk/SculMath/

Symmetry and Pattern: The Art of Oriental Carpets.
http://forum.swarthmore.edu/geometry/rugs/

Tessellation Tutorials. Tutorials teach students how to tessellate (somewhat in the style of M.C. Escher) using HyperCard or HyperStudio, ClarisWorks, LogoWriter, templates, or simple straightedge and compass.
http://forum.swarthmore.edu/sum95/suzanne/tess.intro.html

University of Minnesota Geometry Center Graphics Archive. Includes fractals, digital art, 3-D art, advanced topics such as tilings.
http://www.geom.umn.edu/graphics/

Virtual Polyhedra. Collection of over 1000 virtual-reality polyhedra to explore, with classroom ideas for making and exploring polyhedra.
http://www.li.net/~george/virtual-polyhedra/vp.html

World of Escher. Examples of Escher's work, background, and an annual tesselation contest for students, with winning images.
http://www.worldofescher.com/